Anson Randolph

The changed cross and other religious poems

Anson Randolph

The changed cross and other religious poems

ISBN/EAN: 9783337119010

Printed in Europe, USA, Canada, Australia, Japan

Cover: Foto ©Lupo / pixelio.de

More available books at **www.hansebooks.com**

THE CHANGED CROSS
AND OTHER RELIGIOUS POEMS

PHILADELPHIA
HENRY ALTEMUS

CONTENTS

	PAGE
The Changed Cross,	v
The Meeting Place,	10
"My Times are in Thy Hand,"	13
Wholly Resigned,	15
The Pilgrim,	16
Holy Tears,	19
The Border-Lands,	21
God Our Strength,	23
"All, All is Known to Thee,"	24
Sorrow,	26
Oh! For the Happy Days Gone By,	27
Lost Treasures,	30
Sunday,	34
Mary's Choice,	38
One by One,	39
"Nearer Home,"	41
Religious Hypochondria,	42
Oh! to be Ready,	43
The Bridegroom's Dove,	44
God's Support and Guidance,	48
I Am,	50
God, My Exceeding Joy,	53
A Little While,	55
Hinder Me Not,	57
"I Cling to Thee,"	61

CONTENTS.

	PAGE
Despise Not Thou the Chastening of the Almighty,	62
"Alone, yet not Alone,"	63
Some Murmur When Their Sky is Clear,	64
The School of Suffering,	65
The Prayer of the Righteous,	68
Heaven,	69
A Voice from Heaven,	71
Supplication,	73
Sin,	74
Evening Prayer,	75
A Prayer,	76
The Wandering Heart,	77
"Return Thee to Thy Rest,"	79
Near Jesus,	81
Who is My Brother?	83
My Lambs,	85
The Pilgrim's Wants,	90
The Lord's Prayer,	92
"What is This That He Saith—A Little While?"	93
In Heaven,	95
Pilgrim of Earth,	98
The Cross,	100
"It is I; Be Not Afraid,"	101
Nature and Faith,	103
The Call,	105
God's Anvil,	109
Means and Ends,	110
The Cross and Crown,	111
Oh! My Saviour Crucified,	112
Even Me,	113
The Peace of God,	115

CONTENTS.

	PAGE
Peace,	117
Prayer for Strength,	119
Onward,	121
For the New Year,	123
Dies Iræ,	125
I Would Not Live Alway,	128
Grief was Sent Thee for Thy Good,	131
Guide Me, O Thou Great Jehovah!	132
Just as I Am,	133
Oh! Had I Jubal's Lyre,	134
Thy Will be Done,	135
Nearer, My God, to Thee,	137
Abide With Me,	139
Jesus, Lover of My Soul,	141
Rock of Ages,	143
Angels, Roll the Rock Away!	144
Coronation,	145
Death of a Christian,	146
My Faith Looks Up to Thee,	147
To a Child,	148
When Our Heads are Bowed with Woe,	149
Jesus Only,	150
Nothing but Leaves,	151
Truth,	152
Jesus! the Very Thought of Thee,	153
Christ,	156
Stabat Mater,	158
The Shadow of the Rock,	161
Jerusalem, the Golden,	165
Accepted,	166
Is This All?	167
"Thy Kingdom Come,"	169

	PAGE
Lead, Kindly Light,	171
Jerusalem, My Happy Home,	172
Come to Me!	173
Easter,	174
Unrest,	175
I Sought the Lord,	176
The Voice of Jesus,	177
"Master, Say On!"	178
The Ascension,	181
"Amen,".	183
Sunday Morning Bells,	184
The Master's Call,	185
Veni Creator Spiritus,	186
The Ministry of Song,	187

The Changed Cross.

IT was a time of sadness, and my heart,
Although it knew and loved the better part,
Felt wearied with the conflict and the strife,
And all the needful discipline of life.

And while I thought on these as given to me—
My trial tests of faith and love to be—
It seemed as if I never could be sure
That faithful to the end I should endure.

And thus no longer trusting to His might,
Who says, "we walk by faith and not by sight,"
Doubting, and almost yielding to despair,
The thought arose—My cross I cannot bear.

Far heavier its weight must surely be
Than those of others which I daily see;
Oh! if I might another burden choose,
Methinks I should not fear my crown to lose.

A solemn silence reigned on all around—
E'en Nature's voices uttered not a sound;
The evening shadows seemed of peace to tell,
And sleep upon my weary spirit fell.

A moment's pause, and then a heavenly light
Beamed full upon my wondering, raptured sight;
Angels on silvery wings seemed everywhere,
And angels' music thrilled the balmy air.

Then One, more fair than all the rest to see—
One to whom all the others bowed the knee—
Came gently to me as I trembling lay,
And, "Follow me," He said, "I am the way."

Then speaking thus, He led me far above;
And there, beneath a canopy of love,
Crosses of divers shape and size were seen,
Larger and smaller than my own had been.

And one there was most beauteous to behold—
A little one, with jewels set in gold;

Ah! this, methought, I can with comfort wear,
For it will be an easy one to bear.

And so the little cross I quickly took,
But all at once my frame beneath it shook;
The sparkling jewels fair were they to *see*,
But far too heavy was their *weight* for me.

This may not be, I cried, and looked again,
To see if there was any here could ease my pain;
But one by one I passed them slowly by,
Till on a lovely one I cast my eye;

Fair flowers around its sculptured form entwined,
And grace and beauty seemed in it combined;
Wondering, I gazed, and still I wondered more
To think so many should have passed it o'er.

But, oh! that form so beautiful to see
Soon made its hidden sorrows known to me;

Thorns lay beneath those flowers and colors
    fair:
Sorrowing, I said, "This cross I may not
    bear."

And so it was with each and all around—
Not one to suit my *need* could there be
    found;
Weeping, I laid each heavy burden down,
As my Guide gently said, "No cross, no
    crown!"

At length to Him I raised my saddened
    heart;
He knew its sorrows, bid its doubts depart.
"Be not afraid," He said, "but trust in me—
My perfect love shall now be shown to thee."

And then, with lightened eyes and willing
    feet,
Again I turned, my earthly cross to meet,
With forward footsteps, turning not aside,
For fear some hidden evil might betide.

And there, in the prepared, appointed way—
Listening to hear and ready to obey—
A cross I quickly found of plainest form,
With only words of love inscribed thereon.

With thankfulness I raised it from the rest,
And joyfully acknowledged it the best—
The only one of all the many there
That I could feel was good for me to bear.

And while I thus my chosen one confessed,
I saw a heavenly brightness on it rest;
And as I bent, my burden to sustain,
I recognized my own old cross again!

But, oh! how different did it seem to be
Now I had learned its preciousness to see!
No longer could I unbelieving say,
Perhaps another is a better way.

Ah, no! henceforth my own desire shall be
That He who knows me best should choose for me;
And so whate'er His love sees good to send,
I'll trust it's best, because He knows the end.

"For my thoughts are not your thoughts, saith the Lord."—Isaiah 50:8.

"For I know the thoughts that I think towards you—thoughts of peace, and not of evil, to give you an expected end."—Jer. 29:11.

And when that happy time shall come, of endless peace and rest,
We shall look back upon our path, and say—It was the best.

The Meeting Place.

WHERE the faded flower shall freshen,
Freshen never more to fade;
Where the shaded sky shall brighten,
Brighten never more to shade;
Where the sun-blaze never scorches,
Where the star-beams cease to chill;
Where no tempest stirs the echoes
Of the wood, or wave, or hill;
Where the morn shall wake in gladness,
And the moon the joy prolong;
Where the daylight dies in fragrance
'Mid the burst of holy song—
    Brother, we shall meet and rest
    'Mid the holy and the blest!

Where no shadow shall bewilder,
Where life's vain parade is o'er;
Where the sleep of sin is broken,
And the dreamer dreams no more;
Where the bond is never severed—
Partings, claspings, sobs, and moan,
Midnight waking, twilight weeping,
Heavy noontide—all are done;

THE MEETING PLACE.

Where the child has found its mother,
Where the mother finds the child;
Where dear families are gathered
That were scattered on the wild—
 Brother, we shall meet and rest
 'Mid the holy and the blest!

Where the hidden wound is healed,
Where the blighted light re-blooms;
Where the smitten heart the freshness
Of its buoyant youth resumes;
Where the love that here we lavish
On the withering leaves of time,
Shall have fadeless flowers to fix on,
In an ever spring bright clime;
Where we find the joy of loving,
As we never loved before;
Loving on unchilled, unhindered,
Loving once and evermore—
 Brother, we shall meet and rest
 'Mid the holy and the blest!

Where a blasted world shall brighten
Underneath a bluer sphere,
And a softer, gentler sunshine
Shed its healing splendor here;
Where earth's barren vales shall blossom,

Putting on their robe of green,
And a purer, fairer Eden
Be where only wastes have been;
Where a King in kingly glory,
Such as earth has never known,
Shall assume the righteous sceptre,
Claim and wear the heavenly crown—
    Brother, we shall meet and rest
    'Mid the holy and the blest!

"My Times are in Thy Hand."

PSALM 31 : 15.

FATHER, I know that all my life
   Is portioned out for me;
And the changes that are sure to come
   I do not fear to see:
But I ask Thee for a present mind
   Intent on pleasing Thee.

I ask Thee for a thankful love,
   Through constant watching wise,
To meet the glad with joyful smiles,
   And to wipe the weeping eyes,
And a heart at leisure from itself,
   To soothe and sympathize.

I would not have the restless will
   That hurries to and fro,
Seeking for some great thing to do,
   Or secret thing to know;
I would be dealt with as a child,
   And guided where to go.

Wherever in the world I am,
   In whatsoe'er estate,
I have a fellowship with hearts,
   To keep and cultivate;
And a work of holy love to do,
   For the Lord on whom I wait.

I ask Thee for the daily strength,
   To none that ask denied;
And a mind to blend with outward life,
   While keeping at Thy side,
Content to fill a little space,
   If Thou be glorified.

And if some things I do not ask,
   In my cup of blessing be,
I would have my spirit filled the more
   With grateful love to Thee—
More careful than to serve Thee much,
   To please Thee perfectly.

There are briers besetting every path,
   That call for patient care;
There is a crook in every lot,
   And a need for earnest prayer,
But a lowly heart that leans on Thee,
   Is happy everywhere.

In a service that Thy love appoints,
    There are no bonds for me,
For my secret heart is taught the truth
    That makes Thy children " free,"
And a life of self-renouncing love
    Is a life of liberty.

Wholly Resigned.

CHRIST leads us through no darker rooms
    Than He went through before:
He that into God's kingdom comes,
    Must enter by this door:
Come, Lord, when grace hath made me meet
    Thy blessed face to see,
For if Thy work on earth be sweet,
    What will Thy glory be!

Then I shall end my sad complaints,
    And weary, sinful days;
And join with the triumphant saints,
    That sing Jehovah's praise:
My knowledge of that life is small,
    The eye of faith is dim,
But 'tis enough that Christ knows all,
    And I shall be with Him.

The Pilgrim.

STILL onward through this land of foes
   I pass in Pilgrim guise;
I may not stop to seek repose
   Where cool the shadow lies;
I may not stoop amid the grass
   To pluck earth's fairest flowers,
Nor by her springing fountains pass
   The sultry noontide hours;

Yet flowers I wear upon my breast
   That no earth-garden knows—
White lilies of immortal peace,
   And love's deep-tinted rose;
And there the blue-eyed flowers of faith,
   And hope's bright buds of gold
As lone I tread the upward path,
   In richest hues unfold.

I keep my armor ever on,
   For foes beset my way;
I watch, lest passing on alone
   I fall a helpless prey.

THE PILGRIM.

No earthly love have I—I lean
    Upon no mortal breast;
But my Beloved, though unseen,
    Walks near and gives me rest.

Afar, around, I often see,
    Throughout this desert wide,
His Pilgrims pressing on like me—
    They often pass my side:
The kindly smile, the gentle word,
    For Jesus' sake I give;
But love—O Thou alone adored!
    For Thee alone I live.

Painful and dark the pathway seems
    To distant earthly eyes;
They only see the hedging thorns
    On either side that rise;
They cannot know how soft between
    The flowers of love are strewn—
The sunny ways, the pastures green,
    Where Jesus leads His own;

They cannot see, as darkening clouds
    Behind the Pilgrim close,
How far adown the western glade
    The golden glory flows;

They cannot hear 'mid earthly din
　　The song to Pilgrims known,
Still blending with the angels' hymn
　　Around the wondrous throne.

So I, Thy bounteous token-flowers
　　Still on my bosom wear;
While me, the fleeting love-winged hours
　　To Thee still nearer bear;
So from my lips Thy song shall flow,
　　My sweetest music be;
So on mine eyes the glory grow,
　　Till all is lost in Thee.

Holy Tears.

YES, thou mayst weep, for Jesus shed
    Such tears as those thou sheddest now,
When for the living or the dead,
    Sorrow lay heavy on His brow.

He sees thee weep, yet doth not blame
    The weakness of thy flesh and heart;
Thy human nature is the same
    As that in which He took a part.

He knows its weakness, for He felt
    The crushing power of pain and woe,
How body, soul, and spirit melt
    And faint beneath the stunning blow.

What if poor sinners count thy grief
    The sign of an unchastened will?
He who can give thy soul relief,
    Knows that thou art submissive still.

Turn thee to Him, to Him alone;
    For all that our poor lips can say
To soothe thee, broken-hearted one,
    Would fail to comfort thee to-day.

We will not speak to thee, but sit
   In prayerful silence by thy side:
Grief has its ebbs and flows; 'tis fit
   Our love should wait the ebbing tide.

Jesus Himself will comfort thee,
   In His own time, in His own way;
And haply more than "two or three"
   Unite in prayer for thee to-day.

The Border-Lands.

FATHER, into Thy loving hands
   My feeble spirit I commit,
While wandering in these Border-Lands,
   Until Thy voice shall summon it.

Father, I would not dare to choose
   A longer life, an earlier death;
I know not what my soul might lose
   By shortened or protracted breath.

These Border-Lands are calm and still,
   And solemn are their silent shades;
And my heart welcomes them, until
   The light of life's long evening fades.

I heard them spoken of with dread,
   As fearful and unquiet places;
Shades, where the living and the dead
   Look sadly in each other's faces.

But since Thy hand hath led me here,
   And I have seen the Border-Land;
Seen the dark river flowing near,
   Stood on its brink, as now I stand,

There has been nothing to alarm
    My trembling soul; how could I fear
While thus encircled with Thine arm?
    I never felt Thee half so near.

What should appall me in a place
    That brings me hourly nearer Thee?
When I may almost see Thy face—
    Surely 'tis here my soul would be.

They say the waves are dark and deep,
    That faith has perished in the river;
They speak of death with fear, and weep!
    Shall my soul perish? Never, never.

I know that Thou wilt never leave
    The soul that trembles while it clings
To Thee: I know Thou wilt achieve
    Its passage on Thine out-spread wings.

And since I first was brought so near
    The stream that flows to the Dead Sea,
I think that it has grown more clear
    And shallow than it used to be.

I cannot see the golden gate
    Unfolding yet to welcome me;
I cannot yet anticipate
    The joy of heaven's jubilee.

But I will calmly watch and pray,
　　Until I hear my Saviour's voice,
Calling my happy soul away
　　To see His glory, and rejoice.

God Our Strength.

MAN in his weakness needs a stronger stay
　　Than fellow-men, the holiest and the best:
And yet we turn to them from day to day,
　　As if in them our spirits could find rest.

Gently untwine our childish hands, that cling
　　To such inadequate supports as these,
And shelter us beneath Thy heavenly wing,
　　Till we have learned to walk alone with ease.

Help us, O Lord! with patient love, to bear
　　Each other's faults, to suffer with true meekness;
Help us each other's joys and griefs to share,
　　But let us turn to Thee alone in weakness.

"All, All is Known to Thee."

"When my spirit was overwhelmed within me, then thou knewest my path."

MY GOD, whose gracious pity I may claim,
Calling Thee Father, sweet, endearing name!
The sufferings of this weak and weary frame,
      All, all are known to Thee.

From human eye 'tis better to conceal
Much that I suffer, much I hourly feel;
But oh! the thought does tranquillize and heal,
      All, all is known to Thee.

Each secret conflict with indwelling sin,
Each sickening fear I ne'er the prize shall win,
Each pang from irritation, turmoil, din—
      All, all are known to Thee.

When in the morning unrefreshed I wake,
Or in the night but little sleep can take,
This brief appeal submissively I make—
      All, all is known to Thee.

Nay, all by Thee is ordered, chosen, planned—
Each drop that fills my daily cup; Thy hand
Prescribes for ills none else can understand.
      All, all is known to Thee.

The effectual means to cure what I deplore;
In me Thy longed-for likeness to restore;
Self to dethrone, never to govern more—
      All, all are known to Thee.

And this continued feebleness, this state
Which seems to unnerve and incapacitate,
Will work the cure my hopes and prayers await—
      That can I leave to Thee.

Nor will the bitter draught distasteful prove,
When I recall the SON of Thy dear love
The cup Thou wouldst not for *our* sakes remove—
      That cup He drank for *me*.

He drank it to the dregs—no drop remained
Of wrath, for those whose cup of woe he drained;
Man ne'er can know what that sad cup contained—
      All, all is known to Thee.

And welcome—*precious* can His spirit make
My little drop of suffering for His sake.
Father, the cup I drink, the path I take,
   All, all is known to Thee.

Sorrow.

COUNT each affliction, whether light or grave,
God's messenger sent down to thee; do thou
With courtesy receive him; rise and bow;
And, ere his shadow pass thy threshhold, crave
Permission first his heavenly feet to lave;
Then lay before him all thou hast; allow
No cloud of passion to usurp thy brow
Or mar thy hospitality, no wave
Of mortal tumult to obliterate
Thy soul's marmoreal calmness. Grief should be
Like joy, majestic, equable, sedate,
Confirming, cleansing, raising, making free;
Strong to consume small troubles; to commend
Great thoughts, grave thoughts, thoughts lasting to the end.

Oh! For the Happy Days Gone By.

OH! for the happy days gone by,
   When love ran smooth and free,
Days when my spirit so enjoyed
   More than earth's liberty!

Oh! for the times when on my heart
   Long prayer had never palled,
Times when the ready thought of God
   Would come when it was called!

Then when I knelt to meditate,
   Sweet thoughts came o'er my soul,
Countless, and bright, and beautiful,
   Beyond my own control.

Oh! who hath locked those fountains up?
   Those visions who hath staid?
What sudden act has thus transformed
   My sunshine into shade?

This freezing heart, O Lord! this will
   Dry as the desert sand—
Good thoughts that will not come, bad thoughts
   That come without command—

A faith that seems not faith, a hope
   That cares not for its aim—
A love that none the hotter grows
   At Jesus' blessed name—

The weariness of prayer, the mist
   O'er conscience overspread—
The chill repugnance to frequent
   The feast of angels' bread:

If this drear change be Thine, O Lord!
   If it be Thy sweet will,
Spare not, but to the very brim
   The bitter chalice fill.

But if it hath been sin of mine,
   Oh! show that sin to me—
Not to get back the sweetness lost,
   But to make peace with Thee.

One thing alone, dear Lord! I dread:
   To have a secret spot
That separates my soul from Thee,
   And yet to know it not.

Oh! when the tide of graces set
   So full upon my heart,
I know, dear Lord! how faithlessly
   I did my little part.

I know how well my heart hath earned
   A chastisement like this,
In trifling many a grace away
   In self-complacent bliss.

But if this weariness hath come
   A present from on high,
Teach me to find the hidden wealth
   That in its depths may lie;

So in this darkness I can learn
   To tremble and adore,
To sound my own vile nothingness,
   And thus to love Thee more;

To love Thee, and yet not to think
   That I can love so much;
To have Thee with me, Lord! all day
   Yet not to feel Thy touch.

If I have served Thee, Lord! for hire,
   Hire which Thy beauty showed,
Ah! I can serve Thee now for naught,
   And only as my God.

Oh! blessed be this darkness, then,
   This deep in which I lie,
And blessed be all things that teach
   God's dread supremacy!

Lost Treasures.

LET us be patient, God has taken from us
  The earthly treasures upon which we leaned,
That from the fleeting things which lie around us,
  Our clinging hearts should be forever weaned.

They have passed from us—all our broad possessions:
  Ships, whose white sails flung wide past distant shores;
Lands, whose rich harvests smiled in the glad sunshine;
  Silver and gold, and all our hoarded stores.

And, dearer far, the pleasant home where gathered
  Our loved and loving round the blazing hearth;

Where honored age on the soft cushions rested,
  And childhood played about in frolic mirth:

Where underneath the softened light bent kindly
  The mother's tender glance on daughters fair;
And he on whom all leaned with fond confiding,
  Rested contented from his daily care.

All shipwrecked in one common desolation!
  The garden-walks by other feet are trod;
The clinging vines by other fingers tutored
  To fling their shadows o'er the grassy sod.

While carking care and deep humiliation,
  In tears are mingled with their daily bread;
And the rude blasts we never thought could reach us,
  Have spent their worst on each defenseless head.

Let us be cheerful! The same sky o'er-
arches—
  Soft rain falls on the evil and the good;
On narrow walls, and through our humbler
dwelling,
  God's glorious sunshine pours as rich a
  flood.

Faith, hope, and love still in our hearts
abiding,
  May bear their precious fruits in us the
  same;
And to the couch of suffering we may carry,
  If but the cup of water, in His name.

Let us be thankful, if in this affliction
  No grave is opened for the loving heart;
And while we bend beneath our Father's
chiding,
  We yet can mourn "each family apart."

Shoulder to shoulder let us breast the torrent,
  With not one cold reproach nor angry
  look;
There are some seasons, when the heart is
smitten
  It can no whisper of unkindness brook.

Our life is not in all these brief possessions;
  Our home is not in any pleasant spot;
Pilgrims and strangers we must journey onward,
  Contented with the portion of our lot.

These earthly walls must shortly be dismantled;
  These earthly tents be struck by angel hands;
But to be built up on a sure foundation,
  There, where our Father's mansion ever stands?

There shall we meet, parent and child, and dearer
  That earthly love which makes, half heaven of home;
There shall we find our treasures all awaiting,
  Where change and death and parting never come.

Sunday.

"I was in the spirit on the Lord's day."—Rev. 1 : 10.

AFTER long days of storms and showers,
Of sighing winds, and dripping bowers,
How sweet, at morn, to ope our eyes
On newly "swept and garnished" skies!

To miss the clouds, and driving rain,
And see that all is bright again—
So bright we cannot choose but say,
Is this the world of yesterday?

Even so, methinks, the Sunday brings
A change o'er all familiar things;
A change—we know not whence it came—
They are, and they are not, the same.

There is a spell within, around,
On eye and ear, on sight and sound;
And loath or willing, they and we
Must own this day a mystery.

Sure all things wear a heavenly dress
That sanctifies their loveliness,

Types of that endless resting-day,
When " we shall be changed " as they.

To-day our peaceful, ordered home
Foreshadoweth mansions yet to come;
We foretaste, in domestic love,
The faultless charities above.

And as at yester-eventide
Our tasks and toys were laid aside;
Lo! here our training for the day
When we shall lay them down for aye.

But not alone for musings deep,
Meek souls their " day of days " will keep;
Yet other glorious things than these,
The Christian in his Sabbath sees.

His eyes, by faith, his Lord behold;
How on the week's first day of old,
From hell he rose, on death he trod,
Was seen of men, and went to God.

And as we fondly pause to look
Where in some daily-handled book,
Approval's well-known tokens stand,
Traced by some dear and thoughtful hand;

Even so there shines one day in seven,
Bright with the special mark of heaven,
That we with love and praise may dwell
On Him who loveth us so well.

Whether, in meditative walk,
Alone with God and heaven we talk,
Catching the simple chime that calls
Our feet to some old church's walls;

Or passed within the church's door,
Where poor are rich, and rich are poor,
We say the prayers, and hear the word,
Which there our fathers said and heard;

Or represent in solemn wise,
Our all-prevailing sacrifice;
Feeding in joint communion high,
The life of faith that cannot die.

And surely in a world like this,
So rife with woe, so scant of bliss—
Where fondest hopes are oftenest crossed,
And fondest hopes are severed most;

'Tis something that we kneel and pray
With loved ones near and far away;

SUNDAY.

One God, one faith, one hope, one care,
One form of words, one hour of prayer.

'Tis just—yet pause, till ear and heart,
In one brief silence, ere we part,
Somewhat of that high strain have caught,
"The peace of God which passeth thought."

Then turn we to our earthly homes,
Not doubting but that Jesus comes,
Breathing his peace on hall and hut,
At evening when the doors are shut;

Then speed us on our work-day way,
And hallows every common day;
Without *Him* Sunday's self were dim,
But all are bright, *if spent with Him.*

Mary's Choice.

JESUS, engrave it on my heart,
That thou the one thing needful art;
I could from all things parted be,
But never, never, Lord, from thee.

Needful is thy most precious blood,
Needful is thy correcting rod,
Needful is thy indulgent care,
Needful thy all-prevailing prayer.

Needful thy presence, dearest Lord,
True peace and comfort to afford;
Needful thy promise to impart
Fresh life and vigor to my heart.

Needful art thou to be my stay
Through all life's dark and thorny way;
Nor less in death thou'lt needful be,
To bring my spirit home to thee.

Then needful still, my God, my King,
Thy name eternally I'll sing;
Glory and praise be ever his,
The one thing needful, Jesus is.

One by One.

ONE by one the sands are flowing,
    One by one the moments fall,
Some are coming, some are going—
    Do not strive to grasp them all.

One by one thy duties wait thee,
    Let thy whole strength go to each;
Let no future dreams elate thee;
    Learn thou first what those can teach.

One by one (bright gifts from heaven),
    Joys are sent thee here below;
Take them readily, when given,
    Ready too to let them go.

One by one thy griefs shall meet thee,
    Do not fear an arméd band;
One will fade, while others greet thee,
    Shadows passing through the land.

Do not look at life's long sorrow,
    See how small each moment's pain;
God will help thee for to-morrow—
    Every day begin again.

Every hour that fleets so slowly,
   Has its task to do or bear;
Luminous the crown, and holy,
   If thou set each gem with care.

Do not linger with regretting,
   Or for passion's hour despond,
Nor, the daily toil forgetting,
   Look too eagerly beyond.

Hours are golden links, God's token,
   Reaching heaven but one by one;
Take them lest the chain be broken,
   Ere the pilgrimage be done.

"Nearer Home."

ONE sweetly solemn thought
   Comes to me o'er and o'er:
I'm nearer home to-day
   Than I ever have been before.

Nearer my Father's house,
   Where the many mansions be;
Nearer the great white throne,
   Nearer the jasper sea;

Nearer the bound of life,
   Where we lay our burdens down;
Nearer leaving the cross,
   Nearer wearing the crown.

But lying darkly between,
   Winding down through the night,
Is the dim and unknown stream
   That leads at last to the light.

Closer, closer my steps
   Come to the dark abysm,
Closer, death to my lips
   Presses the awful chrism.

Saviour, perfect my trust,
   Strengthen the might of my faith,
Let me feel as I would when I stand
   On the rock of the shore of death;

Feel as I would when my feet
   Are slipping over the brink;
For it may be I'm nearer home,
   Nearer now, than I think.

Religious Hypochondria.

FORWARD, a step or two, where'er we go
   We gaze not on the spot our feet are treading:
Reading, we look along, or glance below,
   Unconscious of the letters we are reading.
The future moulds the present. Do not halt
To probe, or mourn, each felt or fancied fault;
"Steadfast by faith," who treads where hope hath trod,
Following her winged sister to the throne of God!

Oh! to be Ready.

"OH! to be ready when death shall come,
Oh! to be ready to hasten home!
No earthward clinging, no lingering gaze,
No strife at parting, no sore amaze;
No chains to sever that earth hath twined,
No spell to loosen that love would bind.

"No flitting shadows to dim the light
Of the angel-pinions winged for flight,
No cloud-like phantoms to fling a gloom
'Twixt heaven's bright portals and earth's dark tomb,
But sweetly, gently, to pass away
From the world's dim twilight into day.

"To list the music of angel lyres,
To catch the rapture of seraph fires,
To lean in trust on the risen One,
Till borne away to a fadeless throne;
Oh! to be ready when death shall come,
Oh! to be ready to hasten home!"

The Bridegroom's Dove.

"O MY Dove! in the clefts of the rock, in the secret of the stairs."—CANT. 2:14.

"MY Dove!" The Bridegroom speaks.
　　To whom?
　Whom, think'st thou, meaneth He?
Say, O my soul! canst thou presume
　　He thus addresseth thee?
Yes, 'tis the Bridegroom's voice of love,
Calling thee, O my soul! His Dove!

The Dove is gentle, mild, and meek:
　　Deserve I, then, the name?
I look within in vain to seek
　　Aught which can give a claim:
Yet, made so by redeeming love,
My soul, thou art the Bridegroom's Dove!

Methinks, my soul, that thou may'st see,
　　In this endearing word,
Reasons why Jesus likens thee
　　To this defenceless bird;
Reasons which show the Bridegroom's love
To His poor helpless, timid Dove!

The Dove, of all the feathered tribe,
    Doth least of power possess:
My soul, what better can describe
    Thine utter helplessness?
Yet courage take! the Bridegroom's love
Will keep, defend, protect His Dove!

The Dove hath neither claw nor sting,
    Nor weapon for the fight;
She owes her safety to her wing,
    Her victory to flight.
A shelter hath the Bridegroom's love
Provided for his helpless Dove!

The Hawk comes on, in eager chase—
    The Dove will not resist;
In flying to her hiding-place,
    Her safety doth consist.
The Bridegroom opes his arms of love,
And in them folds His panting Dove!

Nothing the Dove can now molest,
    Safe from the fowler's snare;
The Bridegroom's bosom is her nest—
    Nothing can harm her there.
Encircled by the arms of love,
Almighty power protects the Dove!

As the poor Dove, before the Hawk,
    Quick to her refuge flies,
So need I, in my daily walk,
    The wing which faith supplies
To bear me where the Bridegroom's love
Places beyond all harm His Dove!

My soul of native power bereft,
    To Cavalry repairs:
Immanuel is the *rocky cleft*,
    The secret of the stairs!
Since placed *there* by the Bridegroom's love,
What evil can befall His Dove?

Though Sinai's thunder round her roars,
    Though Ebal's lightnings flash,
Though heaven a fiery torrent pours,
    And riven mountains crash—
Through all, the "still small voice" of love
Whispers, "Be not afraid, my Dove!"

What though the heavens away may pass,
    With fervent heat dissolve,
And round the sun this earthly mass
    No longer shall revolve!
Behold a miracle of love!
The lion quakes, but not the Dove!

My soul, now hid within a rock,
  (The " Rock of Ages " called,)
Amid the universal shock
  Is fearless, unappalled.
A cleft therein, prepared by love,
In safety hides the Bridegroom's Dove!

O happy Dove! thus weak, thus safe;
  Do I resemble her?
Then to my soul, O Lord! vouchsafe
  A *dove-like* character!
Pure, harmless, gentle, full of love,
Make me in spirit, Lord, a Dove!

O Thou who on the Bridegroom's head
  Didst, as a Dove, come down,
Within my soul Thy graces shed,
  Establish there Thy throne;
There shed abroad a Saviour's love,
Thou holy, pure, and heavenly Dove!

God's Support and Guidance.

TRANSLATED FROM THE GERMAN.

FORSAKE me not, my God,
  Thou God of my salvation!
Give me thy light, to be
  My sure illumination.
My soul to folly turns,
  Seeking she knows not what;
Oh! lead her to thyself—
  My God, forsake me not!

Forsake me not, my God!
  Take not thy Spirit from me;
And suffer not the might
  Of sin to o'ercome me.
A father pitieth
  The children he begot;
My Father, pity me—
  My God, forsake me not.

Forsake me not, my God,
  Thou God of life and power,
Enliven, strengthen me
  In every evil hour;

And when the sinful fire
   Within my heart is hot,
Be not thou far from me—
   My God, forsake me not!

Forsake me not, my God!
   Uphold me in my going,
That evermore I may
   Please thee in all well-doing;
And that thy will, O Lord!
   May never be forgot
In all my works and ways—
   My God, forsake me not!

Forsake me not, my God!
   I would be thine forever;
Confirm me mightily
   In every right endeavor:
And when my hour is come,
   Cleansed from all stain and **spot**
Of sin, receive my soul—
   My God, forsake me not!

I Am.

"God calls himself I Am, leaving a blank which each soul may fill up with that which is most precious to himself."

THOU bid'st us call, and giv'st us many a name,
  That thou may'st hear and answer every cry;
But—for the wants of all are not the same—
  Another name thy wondrous love did try;
To Moses first thou gav'st it, and he knew
Its worth, and taught us how to prize it, too.
I Am—let every sinner kneel, and thank
The Lord, and with his wants fill up the blank.
Thy very wounds do say, each drop they bleed,
  "I am thy need."

Oh! I am weary of this life,
  Of all its vanity and care;
Where can I hide me from its strife,
  From all its noises—where?

My spirit sinks beneath the load,
I pant to reach a safe abode.
When shall I find a sweet release?
Remains there yet a lasting peace,
A calm from my long storm-tost breast?
    "I Am thy rest."

Oh! I am full of grievous sin,
   I can do naught that's right;
O God! how base my soul is in
   Thy pure and holy sight!
Thy perfect laws I daily, hourly break,
And will not yield my will for thy sweet sake.
Still in my soul do burn wicked desires,
And my heart's altar bears unhallowed fires;
I can do naught but all these things confess.
    "I Am thy righteousness."

But, Lord, I am so weak, so weak,
   I cannot stand before thy face,
Thy praises I can hardly speak,
   Hardly stretch forth my hands for grace;
The way seems long, the burden who can bear?
Lord, must I sink beneath the load of care?
Thus is it now, what shall it be at length?
    "I Am thy strength."

Lord, I must die; e'en now the wing
  Of thy dread angel hovereth nigh;
I know the message he doth bring—
  "Soul, thou hast sinned, and thou must
    die."
All nature feels and owns the just decree,
And is this all that is in store for me—
Ashes to ashes, dust to kindred dust,
No hope, no light? Surely my spirit must
Sink in despair ere nature's last, fierce
    strife—
  "I Am thy life."

Oh! wonderful thou art!
  Too wonderful for me is such great love,
Shining in such a heart
  Like sunbeams from above.
How rich am I! yea, all things I possess,
  Peace, joy, life, strength, and perfect
righteousness.
Jehovah shows himself, and gives to me
All my desire. Look, trembling soul, and
  see
On what a treasury thy want may call—
  "I Am thine all in all."

God, My Exceeding Joy.

PSALM 43 : 4.

I.

EARLY my spirit turned
  From earthly things away,
And agonized and yearned
  For the eternal day :
Dimly I saw, when but a boy,
  God, my exceeding joy.

II.

In days of fiercer flame,
  When passion urged me on,
'Twas only bliss in name—
  The pleasure soon was gone.
Compared with thee, how all things cloy,
  God, my exceeding joy.

III.

At length the moment came—
  Jesus made known his love;
High shot the kindling flame
  To glories all above.
Now all the powers one theme employ,
  God, my exceeding joy.

IV.

Shadows came on apace;
  Tears were a pensive shower;
I cried for timely grace
  To save me from the hour:
Thou gavest peace without alloy,
  God, my exceeding joy.

V.

One trial yet awaits,
  Gigantic at the close;
All that my spirit hates
  May then my peace oppose;
But God shall this last foe destroy,
  God, my exceeding joy.

A Little While.

BEYOND the smiling and the weeping
    I shall be soon;
Beyond the waking and the sleeping,
Beyond the sowing and the reaping,
    I shall be soon.
  Love, rest, and home!
  Sweet hope!
  Lord, tarry not, but come.

Beyond the blooming and the fading
    I shall be soon;
Beyond the shining and the shading,
Beyond the hoping and the dreading,
    I shall be soon.
  Love, rest, and home!
  Sweet hope!
  Lord, tarry not, but come.

Beyond the rising and the setting
    I shall be soon;
Beyond the calming and the fretting,
Beyond remembering and forgetting,
    I shall be soon.
  Love, rest, and home!
  Sweet hope!
  Lord, tarry not, but come.

Beyond the gathering and the strewing
   I shall be soon;
Beyond the ebbing and the flowing,
Beyond the coming and the going,
   I shall be soon.
  Love, rest, and home!
  Sweet hope!
  Lord, tarry not, but come.

Beyond the parting and the meeting
   I shall be soon;
Beyond the farewell and the greeting,
Beyond this pulse's fever beating,
   I shall be soon.
  Love, rest, and home!
  Sweet hope!
  Lord, tarry not, but come.

Beyond the frost-chain and the fever
   I shall be soon;
Beyond the rock-waste and the river,
Beyond the ever and the never,
   I shall be soon.
  Love, rest, and home!
  Sweet hope.
  Lord, tarry not, but come.

Hinder Me Not.

HINDER me not! the path is long and weary,
   I may not pause nor tarry by the way,
Night cometh, when no man may journey onward,
   For we must walk as children of the day.

I know the city lieth fair behind me,
   The very brightest gem that studs the plain,
But thick and fast the lurid clouds are rising,
   Which soon shall scatter into fiery rain.

I must press on until I reach my Zoar,
   And there find refuge from the fearful blast:
In thy cleft side, O smitten Saviour! hide me,
   Till the calamity be overpast.

Ye cannot tempt me back with pomp or pleasure,
   All in my eager grasp have turned to dust;

The shield of love around my hearth is broken,
  How shall I place on man's frail life my trust?

But my heart lingers when I pass the dwellings,
  Where children play about the open door;
And pleasant voices waken up the echoes,
  From silent lips of those I see no more.

For through their chambers swept the solemn warning,
  Arise! depart! for this is not your rest;
They folded their pale hands and sought the presence—
  I only bore the arrow in my breast.

But there is balm in Gilead, and a Healer
  Whose sovereign power can cure our every ill;
And to the soul, more wildly tempest tossing
  Than ever Galilee, say, Peace, be still!

Who showing his own name thereon engraven,
  With bleeding hands will draw the dart again,

And whisper: "Should the true disciple
    murmur
  To taste the cup his Master's lip could
    drain?"

And then lead on, until we reach the river,
  Which all must cross, and some must
    cross alone;
Oh! ye who in the land of peace are wearied,
  How shall ye breast the Jordan's swelling
    moan?

I know not if the wave shall rage or slumber,
  When I shall stand upon the nearer shore.
But one whose form the Son of God resembleth,
  Will cross with me, and I shall ask no
    more.

O weary heads! rest on your Saviour's
    bosom,
  O weary feet! press on the path he trod,
O weary souls! your rest shall be remaining
  When ye have gained the city of your
    God!

O glorious city! jasper built, and shining
  With God's own glory in effulgent light,
Wherein no manner of defilement cometh,
  Nor any shadow flung from passing night.

Then shall ye pluck fruits from that tree immortal,
  And be like gods, but find no curse therein.
There shall ye slake your thirst in that full fountain
  Whose distant streams sufficed to cleanse your sin.

There shall ye find your dead in Christ arisen,
  And learn from them to sing the angel's song;
Well may ye echo from earth's waiting prison,
  The martyr's cry: "How long, O Lord! how long!"

"I Cling to Thee."

O HOLY Saviour! Friend unseen!
Since on thine arm thou bidst me lean,
Help me through life's varying scene,
    By faith I cling to Thee.

Blest with this fellowship divine,
Take what thou wilt, I'll ne'er repine;
E'en as the branches to the vine,
    My soul would cling to Thee.

Far from her home, fatigued, oppressed,
Here has she found her place of rest,
An exile still, yet not unblessed,
    While she can cling to Thee.

What though the world deceitful prove,
And earthly friends and joys remove,
With patient uncomplaining love,
    Still would I cling to Thee.

Though faith and hope may long be tried,
I ask not, need not aught beside;
How safe, how calm, how satisfied,
    The soul that clings to Thee.

They fear not Satan nor the grave;
They feel Thee near, and strong to save;
Nor dread to cross e'en Jordan's wave,
    Because they cling to Thee.

Blest is my lot—whate'er befall;
What can disturb me—who appall?
While as my strength, my rock, my all,
    Saviour! I cling to Thee.

Despise Not Thou the Chastening of the Almighty.

THE Sunshine to the flower may give
    The tints that charm the sight,
But scentless would that floweret live
    If skies were always bright;
Dark clouds and showers its scent bestow,
And purest joy is born of woe.

He who each bitter cup rejects,
    No living spring shall quaff;
He whom thy rod in love corrects,
    Shall lean upon thy staff:
Happy, thrice happy, then, is he
Who knows his chastening is from thee.

"Alone, yet not Alone."

WHEN no kind earthly friend is near,
With gentle words my heart to cheer,
Still am I with my Saviour dear;
   "Alone, yet not alone."

Though no loved forms my path attend,
With tender looks o'er me to bend,
Yet am I with my unseen Friend;
   "Alone, yet not alone."

When sorely racked with pain and grief,
Here I can find a sure relief;
And I rejoice in the belief:
   "Alone, yet not alone."

'Tis on his strength that I rely,
And doubts and fears at once defy;
So happy, so content am I,
   "Alone, yet not alone."

E'en when with friends my lot is cast,
And words of love are flowing fast,
Still am I when those hours are past,
   "Alone, yet not alone."

If all my earthly friends remove,
My fondest wishes empty prove,

Still am I with my Saviour's love,
   "Alone, yet not alone."

Whate'er may now to me betide,
I have a place wherein to hide;
By faith, 'tis e'en at his blest side;
   "Alone, yet not alone."

Some Murmur When Their Sky is Clear.

SOME murmur when their sky is clear
 And wholly bright to view,
If one small speck of dark appear
 In their great heaven of blue:
And some with thankful love are filled,
 If but one streak of light,
One ray of God's good mercy, gild
 The darkness of their night.

In palaces are hearts that ask,
 In discontent and pride,
Why life is such a weary task,
 And all good things denied:
And hearts in poorest huts admire
 How Love has in their aid—
Love that not ever seems to tire—
 Such rich provision made.

The School of Suffering.

SAVIOUR, beneath thy yoke,
  My wayward heart doth pine;
All unaccustomed to the stroke
  Of love divine:
Thy chastisements, my God, are hard to bear,
Thy cross is heavy for frail flesh to wear.

"Perishing child of clay!
  Thy sighing I have heard;
Long have I marked thy evil way,
  How thou hast erred!
Yet fear not, by my own most holy name
I will shed healing through thy sin-sick frame."

Praise to thee, gracious Lord!
  I fain would be at rest;
Oh! now fulfill thy faithful word
  And make me blest;
My soul would lay her heavy burden down
And take, with joyfulness, the promised crown.

"Stay, thou short-sighted child!
  There is much first to do,
Thy heart so long by sin defiled,
  I must renew;
Thy will must here be taught to bend to mine,
Or the sweet peace of heaven can ne'er be
  thine."

Yea, Lord, but thou canst soon
  Perfect thy work in me,
Till like the pure, calm summer noon
  I shine by thee;
A moment shine, that all thy power may
  trace,
Then pass in stillness to my heavenly place.

"Ah! coward soul, confess
  Thou shrinkest from my cure,
Thou tremblest at the sharp distress
  Thou must endure;
The foes on every hand for war arrayed,
The thorny path in tribulation laid.

"The process slow of years,
  The discipline of life;
Of outward woes and secret tears,
  Sickness and strife;
Thine idols taken from thee one by one,
Till thou canst dare to live with me alone.

"Some gentle souls there are,
Who yield unto my love,
Who, ripening fast beneath my cure,
I soon remove;
But thou stiff-necked art, and hard to rule;
Thou must stay longer in affliction's school."

My Maker and my King!
Is this thy love to me?
Oh! that I had the lightning's wing,
From earth to flee;
How can I bear the heavy weight of woes
Thine indignation on the creature throws?

"Thou canst not, O my child!
So hear my voice again;
I will bear all thy anguish wild,
Thy grief—thy pain;
My arms shall be around thee, day by day,
My smile shall cheer thee on thy heavenward way.

"In sickness I will be
Watching beside thy bed,
In sorrow thou shalt lean on me
Thy aching head;
In every struggle thou shalt conqueror prove,
Nor death itself shall sever from my love."

O grace beyond compare!
  O love most high and pure!
Saviour begin, no longer spare,
  I can endure;
Only vouchsafe thy grace, that I may **live**
Unto thy glory who canst so forgive.

The Prayer of the Righteous.

WHEN thy best efforts fail, when day by day
  Thy heart grows sick of hope deferred, and still
  New obstacles arise, and omens ill
Threaten thy future, art thou moved to pray?
'Tis well the good incentive to obey.
  Pray for a confirmation of thy will
  In fealty to duty—to fulfill
All her behests till she commands to stay
The strife—from unavailing toil to rest.
  But with all precious benefits of prayer—
  Peace, strengthened purpose, fortitude to bear
Life's evils, thou shalt be most richly blest
  If, all thy heart's desires comprised in one,
  Thou art content to pray—"THY WILL BE DONE."

Heaven.

OH! heaven is nearer than mortals think,
    When they look with a trembling dread
At the misty future that stretches on,
    From the silent home of the dead.

'Tis no lone isle on a boundless main,
    No brilliant but distant shore,
Where the lovely ones who are called away
    Must go to return no more.

No, heaven is near us; the mighty veil
    Of mortality blinds the eye,
That we cannot see the angel bands,
    On the shores of eternity.

The eye that shuts in a dying hour
    Will open the next in bliss;
The welcome will sound in the heavenly world,
    Ere the farewell is hushed in this.

We pass him the clasp of mourning friends,
    To the arms of the loved and lost,
And those smiling faces will greet us there,
    Which on earth we have valued most.

Yet oft in the hours of holy thought,
    To the thirsting soul is given
That power to pierce through the mist of
    sense,
    To the beauteous scenes of heaven.

Then very near seem its pearly gates,
    And sweetly its harpings fall,
Till the soul is restless to soar away,
    And longs for the angel's call.

I know when the silver cord is loosed,
    When the veil is rent away,
Not long and dark shall the passage be,
    To the realm of endless day.

A Voice from Heaven.

I SHINE in the light of God,
   His image stamps my brow;
Through the shadows of Death my feet have
    trod,
   And I reign in glory now.
No breaking heart is here,
   No keen and thrilling pain,
No wasted cheek, where the burning tear
   Hath rolled, and left its stain.

I have found the joys of heaven,
   I am one of the angel band;
To my head a crown is given,
   And a harp is in my hand;
I have learned the song they sing,
   Whom Jesus hath made free,
And the glorious walls of heaven still ring
   With my new-born melody.

No sin, no grief, no pain—
   Safe in my happy home;
My fears all fled, my doubts all slain,
   My hour of triumph come;

O friends of my mortal years!
    The trusted and the true,
You're walking still the vale of tears,
    But I wait to welcome you.

Do I forget? Oh, no!
    For memory's golden chain
Shall bind my heart to the hearts below,
    Till they meet and touch again;
Each link is strong and bright,
    While love's electric flame
Flows freely down, like a river of light,
    To the world from whence I came.

Do you mourn when another star
    Shines out from the glorious sky?
Do you weep when the voice of war
    And the rage of conflict die?
Why then should your tears roll down,
    Or your heart be sorely riven,
For another gem in the Saviour's crown,
    And another soul in heaven?

Supplication.

LORD, hear my prayer!
Turn not thine ear from my distress,
But with thy loving mercy bless,
   Lest I despair.

Be gracious, Lord!
My soul is oft opprest and weak;
Oh! aid me when I comfort seek
   In thy blest word.

My footsteps stray;
I wander often from the road
That leads to peace and thee my God;
   Teach thou the way.

Oh! make me pure,
Clothe thou my soul in spotless white,
That my acceptance in thy sight
   Be always sure.

Let me be one
Of all the sinless company
That round thy throne hosannahs sing,
   Through Christ thy Son.

Thy will be done
On earth, as by each holy one,
Thy own redeemed, who near thy throne
  Bow down the knee!

Sin.

IF I have sinned in act, I may repent;
  If I have erred in thought, I may disclaim
  My silent error, and yet feel no shame;
But if my soul, big with an ill intent,
Guilty in will, by fate be innocent,
  Or being bad yet murmurs at the curse
  And incapacity of being worse,
That makes my hungry passion still keep Lent
In keen expectance of a Carnival,—
  Where, in all worlds that round the sun revolve
And shed their influence on this passive ball,
  Abides a power that can my soul absolve?
Could any sin survive and be forgiven
One sinful wish would make a hell of heaven.

Evening Prayer.

FATHER of mercy! at the close of day,
My work and duties done, to thee I pray
    Before I sleep;
With clasped hands I humbly bow my head,
And ask thee, Lord, ere I retire to bed,
    My soul to keep.

The sins and failings of the day now past,
The shadows on my soul that they have cast,
    Do thou forgive;
Oh! purge my life from every taint of sin,
That I within thy courts may enter in,
    With thee to live.

Whatever sorrow I this day have known,
I spread it now, O Lord! before thy throne—
    Oh! succor send;
I would beneath thy chastening hand be still,
And meekly bow before thy sovereign will,
    Unto the end.

And now with folded hand upon my breast,
At peace with thee, I lay me down to rest
    Upon my bed;
May angels guard me through the darksome night,
From troubled dreams, until the morning light
    Its beams shall shed.

A Prayer.

Imitated from the Persian.

LORD! who art merciful as well as just,
Incline thine ear to me, a child of dust!
  Not what I would, O Lord! I offer thee,
    Alas! but what I can.
  Father Almighty, who hast made me man,
And bade me look to heaven, for thou art there,
  Accept my sacrifice and humble prayer.
Four things which are not in thy treasury,
I lay before thee, Lord, with this petition:
    My nothingness, my wants,
    My sins, and my contrition.

The Wandering Heart.

ALAS! for the wildly wandering heart,
   And its changing idol guests,
It has roamed away to the world's far ends
   At the vagrant wind's behests;
More fleet in its course than the flying dart—
   Alas! for the wandering heart.

Go, bind it with memory's holiest spells,
   But it recks not the things of old;
Go, chain it in gratitude's surest cells,
   With fetters more precious than gold;
Yet ever, oh! ever, it will depart—
   Alas! for the wandering heart.

Is it gone up to listen at heaven's gate,
   To Gabriel's lyre of praise,
And to catch the deep chanting where seraphs wait,
   As a lesson for its mortal lays?
Oh! no, for it loves from such lessons to part—
   Alas! for the wandering heart.

It loves on a worthless and treacherous
    world
  To bestow its high desires,
And the lamp which it ought to be lighting
    in heaven
  It kindles at idol fires;
Full seldom it turns to its guiding chart—
  Alas! for the wandering heart.

It needs to be steeped in the briny wave
  Of affliction's billowy sea,
And salt tears must water its way to the
    grave,
  Ere it will from these vanities flee;
It must ever be feeling the chastening
    smart—
  Alas! for the wandering heart.

My Father! my Father! this heart would be
    thine!
  Restore from its wanderings;
Oh! visit and nourish thy wilderness vine,
  Though it be from the bitter springs:
Till the years of its pruning in time shall be
    o'er,
And its shoots in eternity wander no more!

"Return Thee to Thy Rest."

RETURN, return thee to thine only rest,
   Lone pilgrim of the world!
   Far erring from the fold—
By the dark night and risen storms distressed:
List, weary lamb, the Shepherd's anxious voice,
And once again within his arms rejoice.

Return, return, thy fair white fleece is soiled
   And by sharp briers rent—
   Thy little strength is spent;
Yet he will pity thee, thou torn and spoiled.
There, thou art cradled on his tender breast;
Now never more, sweet lamb, forsake that rest.

Return, return, my soul; be like this lamb;
   Yet can it, can it be
   That thou should'st pardon me,
Thou injured love! all ingrate as I am;
Once again, weary of earth's trifling things,
False as the desert's far and shining springs?

Return, return to thy forsaken Friend,
   So long despised, forgot—
That now thou wandering heart, 'twere just
   If he should "know thee not:"
Yet on, press on, towards the mercy-seat,
And if thou perish, perish at his feet.

Return, return, for he is near thee dwelling,
   And not into the air
   Need rise the sighs of prayer;
Into his ear thou'rt all thy sorrows telling;
Thou need'st not speak to him through spaces wide—
For he is near thee, even at thy side.

"Him have I pierced"—oh! I come, I come;
   My heart is broken, Lord,
   It needs nor voice nor word;
One only look brought Peter back of yore;
How bitterly I weep as then he wept!
Henceforth, oh! keep me, and I shall be kept.

Near Jesus.

I WANT to live near Jesus,
   And never go astray,
To feel that I am growing
   More like Him every day;
That I am always laying
   My treasure up above,
And gaining more the spirit
   Of His gentleness and love.

I want such steadfast purpose
   My mission to fulfill,
That it may be my meat and drink,
   To do my Father's will,
To follow in His footsteps,
   Who never turned aside
From the path that leads to Heaven
   Though often sorely tried.

Oh! that in His humility
   My spirit may be clad!
That I may have the patience
   My suffering Saviour had,

A heart more disengaged
   From earth and earthly things,
Which through life's varied trials
   To Jesus simply clings.

Oh! I shall live near Jesus
   And never go astray,
And every sin-defiling stain
   Shall soon be washed away;
And I'll bear my Master's image
   When I see Him face to face,
Then earth shall lose the power
   Its brightness to deface.

Who is My Brother?

MUST I my brother keep,
   And share his pains and toil,
And weep with those that weep,
   And smile with those that smile
And act to each a brother's part,
And feel his sorrows in my heart?

Must I his burden bear,
   As though it were my own,
And do as I would care
   Should to myself be done,
And faithful to his interests prove,
And as myself my neighbor love?

Must I reprove his sin,
   Must I partake his grief,
And kindly enter in
   And minister relief—
The naked clothe, the hungry feed,
And love him not in word, but deed?

Then, Jesus, at thy feet,
   A student let me be,

And learn, as it is meet,
　　My duty, Lord, of thee;
For thou didst come on mercy's plan,
And all thy life was love to man.

Oh! make me as thou art,
　　Thy spirit, Lord, bestow—
The kind and gentle heart
　　That feels another's woe,
That thus I may be like my Head,
And in my Saviour's footsteps tread.

My Lambs.

I LOVED them so,
That when the elder Shepherd of the fold
Came, covered with the storm, and pale and cold,
And begged for one of my sweet lambs to hold,
I bade him go.

He claimed the pet;
A little fondling thing, that to my breast
Clung always, either in quiet or unrest;
I thought of all my lambs I loved him best,
And yet—and yet—

I laid him down,
In those white, shrouded arms, with bitter tears;
For some voice told me that, in after-years,
He should know naught of passion, grief, or fears,
As I had known.

And yet again
That elder Shepherd came; my heart grew
  faint;
He claimed another lamb, with sadder plaint,
Another! She who, gentle as a saint,
  Ne'er gave me pain.

Aghast I turned away;
There sat she, lovely as an angel's dream,
Her golden locks with sunlight all agleam,
Her holy eyes with heaven in their beam:
  I knelt to pray:

"Is it thy will?
My Father, say, must this pet lamb be given?
Oh! thou hast many such, dear Lord, in
  heaven;"
And a soft voice said: "Nobly hast thou
  striven;
  But—peace, be still."

Oh! how I wept,
And clasped her to my bosom, with a wild
And yearning love—my lamb, my pleasant
  child:
Her, too, I gave; the little angel smiled,
  And slept.

"Go! go!" I cried:
For once, again, that Shepherd laid his hand
Upon the noblest of our household band:
Like a pale spectre, there he took his stand,
    Close to his side.

    And yet how wondrous sweet
The look with which he heard my passionate cry:
"Touch not my lamb; for him oh! let me die!"
"A little while," he said, with smile and sigh,
    "Again to meet."

    Hopeless I fell;
And when I rose, the light had burned so low,
So faint, I could not see my darling go:
He had not bidden me farewell; but oh!
    I felt farewell

    More deeply, far,
Than if my arms had compassed that slight frame;
Though could I but have heard him call my name—

"Dear mother"—but in heaven 'twill be the
    same;
    There burns my star!

    He will not take
Another lamb, I thought, for only one
Of the dear fold is spared to be my sun,
My guide, my mourner when this life is
    done;
    My heart would break.

    Oh! with that thrill
I heard him enter; but I did not know
(For it was dark) that he had robbed me so;
The idol of my soul!—he could not go—
    O heart! be still!

    Came morning: can I tell
How this poor frame its sorrowful tenant
    kept?
For waking tears were mine; I, sleeping,
    wept,
And days, months, years, that weary vigil
    kept.
    Alas! "Farewell."

How often it is said!
I sit and think, and wonder too, sometime,
How it will seem when, in that happier
   clime,
It never will ring out like funeral chime
      Over the dead.

No tears! no tears!
Will there a day come that I shall not
   weep?
For I bedew my pillow in my sleep.
Yes, yes; thank God! no grief that clime
      shall keep—
   No weary years.

Ay! it is well!
Well with my lambs, and with their earthly
   guide;
There, pleasant rivers wander they beside,
Or strike sweet harps upon its silver tide—
      Ay! it is well.

Through the dreary day
They often come from glorious light to me;
I cannot feel their touch, their faces see,
Yet my soul whispers, they do come to me;
      Heaven is not far away.

The Pilgrim's Wants.

I WANT that adorning divine,
    Thou, only, my God, canst bestow;
I want in those beautiful garments to shine,
    Which distinguish thy household below.
                  [Col. 3 : 12-17.]

I want, oh! I want to attain
    Some likeness, my Saviour, to thee:
That longed-for resemblance once more to
    regain,
    Thy comeliness put upon me.
                    [1 John 3 : 2, 3.]

I want to be marked for thy own;
    Thy seal on my forehead to wear;
To receive that "new name" on the mystic
    white stone,
    Which only thyself canst declare.
                    [Rev. 2 : 17.]

I want, every moment, to feel
    That the Spirit does dwell in my heart;

That his power is present to cleanse and to
  heal,
 And newness of life to impart.
    [Rom. 8: 11–16.]

I want so in thee to abide,
 As to bring forth some fruit to thy praise;
The branch that thou prunest, though feeble
  and dried,
 May languish, but never decays.
    [John 15: 2–5.]

I want thine own hand to unbind
 Each tie to terrestrial things,
Too tenderly cherished, too closely entwined,
 Where my heart too tenaciously clings.
    [1 John 2: 15.]

I want, by my aspect serene,
 My actions and words, to declare
That my treasure is placed in a country un-
  seen,
 That my heart and affections are there.
    [Matt. 6: 19–21.]

I want, as a traveller, to haste
 Straight onward, nor pause on my way;

No forethought or anxious contrivance to
 waste
　On my tent, only pitched for a day.
　　　　　　　　　　　[Heb. 13: 5, 6.]

I want (and this sums up my prayer)
　To glorify thee till I die;
Then calmly to yield up my soul to thy
 care,
　And breathe out in prayer my last sigh.
　　　　　　　　　　　[Phil. 3: 8, 9.]

The Lord's Prayer.

OUR Father which in heaven art,
　We sanctify thy name;
Thy kingdom come: thy will be done:
　In heaven and earth the same:
Give us this day our daily bread:
　And us forgive thou so,
As we on them that us offend
　Forgiveness do bestow:
Into temptation lead us not,
　But us from evil free:
For thine the kingdom, power, and praise
　Is, and shall ever be.

"What is This That He Saith—A Little While?"

John 16 : 18.

OH! for the peace which floweth as a river,
  Making Life's desert-places bloom and smile;
Oh! for a faith to grasp Heaven's bright "forever"
  Amid the shadows of Earth's "little while."

"A little while" for patient vigil-keeping,
  To face the storm, to wrestle with the strong;
"A little while" to sow the seed with weeping,
  Then bind the sheaves and sing the harvest-song.

"A little while" to wear the robe of sadness,
  To toil with weary step through erring ways;
Then to pour forth the fragrant oil of gladness,
  And clasp the girdle of the robe of praise.

"A little while" 'mid shadow and illusion
  To strive by faith Love's mysteries to
    spell;
Then read each dark enigma's clear solution,
  Then hail Light's verdict—"He doeth all
    things well."

"A little while" the earthen pitcher taking
  To wayside brooks from far-off fountains
    fed;
Then the parched lip its thirst forever slaking
  Beside the fullness of the Fountain Head.

"A little while" to keep the oil from failing,
  "A little while" Faith's flickering lamp to
    trim,
And then the Bridegroom's coming footstep
    hailing,
  To haste to meet him with the bridal
    hymn.

And He who is at once both Gift and Giver,
  The future Glory, and the present smile,
With the bright promise of the glad "forever,"
  Will light the shadows of the "little
    while."

In Heaven.

"Their angels do always behold the face of my Father."

SILENCE filled the courts of Heaven,
Hushed were seraphs' harp and tone,
When a little new-born seraph
Knelt before the Eternal Throne;
While its soft white hands were lifted,
Clasped as if in earnest prayer,
And its voice in dove-like murmurs
Rose like music on the air.
Light from the full fount of Glory
On his robes of whiteness glistened,
And the bright-winged seraphs near him
Bowed their radiant heads and listened.

"Lord from Thy Throne of Glory here
    My heart turns fondly to another,
O Lord, our God, the Comforter!
    Comfort, comfort, *my sweet Mother!*
Many sorrows hast Thou sent her,
    Meekly has she drained the cup,
And the jewels Thou hast lent her
    Unrepining yielded up.
        Comfort, comfort, *my sweet Mother!*

"Earth is growing lonely round her;
    Friend and lover hast Thou taken;
Let her not, though woes surround her,
    Feel herself by Thee forsaken;
Let her think, when faint and weary,
    We are waiting for her *here;*
Let each loss that makes earth dreary
    Make the hope of Heaven more dear.
        Comfort, comfort, *my sweet Mother!*

"Thou who once, in nature human,
    Dwelt on earth a little child,
Pillowed on the breast of Woman,
    Blessed Mary! undefiled.
Thou who from the cross of suffering,
    Marked Thy Mother's tearful face,
And bequeathed her to Thy loved one,
    Bidding him to fill Thy place.
        Comfort, comfort, *my sweet Mother!*

"Thou who once from Heaven descending
    Tears and woes and conflicts won,
Thou who nature's laws suspending
    Gav'st the widow back her son,
Thou who at the grave of Lazarus
    Wept with those who wept their dead,

Thou! who once in mortal anguish
   Bowed Thine own anointed head.
      Comfort, comfort, *my sweet Mother!*"

The dove-like murmurs died away
   Upon the radiant air,
But still the little suppliant knelt
   With hands still clasped in prayer;
Still were those mildly pleading eyes
   Turned to the sapphire throne,
Till golden harp and angel voice
   Rang forth in mingled tone,
And as the swelling numbers flowed
   By angel voices given,
Rich, sweet, and clear, the anthem rolled
   Through all the courts of Heaven.
" He is the widow's God," it said,
   Who spared not " His own Son."
The infant cherub bowed his head—
   " Thy will, *O Lord! be* done."

Pilgrim of Earth.

PILGRIM of earth, who art journeying to heaven!
  Heir of Eternal Life! Child of the day!
Cared for, watched over, beloved and forgiven—
  Art thou discouraged because of the way?

Cared for, watched over, though often thou seemest
  Justly forsaken, nor counted a child;
Loved and forgiven, though rightly thou deemest
  Thyself all unlovely, impure, and defiled.

Weary and thirsty—no water-brook near thee,
  Press on, nor faint at the length of the way.
The God of thy life will assuredly hear thee—
  He will provide thee strength for the day.

Break through the brambles and briers that
  obstruct thee,
 Dread not the gloom and the blackness of
  night,
Lean on the hand that will safely conduct
  thee,
 Trust to His eye to whom darkness is
  light.

Be trustful, be steadfast, whatever betide
  thee,
 Only one thing do thou ask of the Lord—
Grace to go forward wherever He guide thee,
 Simply believing the truth of His word.

Still on thy spirit deep anguish is pressing,
 Not for the yoke that His wisdom be-
  stows:
A heavier burden thy soul is distressing,
 A heart that is slow in His love to repose.

Earthliness, coldness, unthankful behavior—
 Ah! thou mayest sorrow, but do not de-
  spair;
Even this grief thou mayest bring to thy
  Saviour;
 Cast upon Him e'en this burden and care!

Bring all thy hardness—His power can sub-
　　due it;
　How full is the promise! The blessing
　　how free!
"Whatsoever ye ask, in my name, I will
　　do it,
　Abide in my love, and be joyful in me."

The Cross.

TREE, which Heaven has willed to dower
With that true fruit whence we live,
As that other, death did give;
Of new Eden loveliest flower;
Bow of light, that in worst hour
Of the worst flood signal true
O'er the world, of mercy threw;
Fair plant, yielding sweetest wine;
Of our David harp divine:
Of our Moses tables new;
Sinner am I, therefore I
Claim upon thy mercies make,
Since alone for sinners' sake
God on thee endured to die.

"It Is I; Be Not Afraid."

MATTHEW 14 : 27.

TOSSED with rough winds, and faint with fear,
Above the tempest, soft and clear,
What still small accents greet mine ear?
"'Tis I; be not afraid.

"'Tis I, who led thy steps aright;
'Tis I, who gave thy blind eyes sight;
'Tis I, thy Lord, thy Life, thy Light:
'Tis I; be not afraid.

"These raging winds, this surging sea,
Bear not a breath of wrath to thee;
That storm has all been spent on Me:
'Tis I; be not afraid.

"This bitter cup fear not to drink;
I know it well—oh! do not shrink,
I tasted it o'er Kedron's brink:
'Tis I; be not afraid.

"Mine eyes are watching by thy bed,
　Mine arms are underneath thy head,
　My blessing is around thee shed:
　　　　'Tis I; be not afraid.

"When on the other side thy feet
　Shall rest 'mid thousand welcomes sweet,
　One well-known voice thy heart shall greet;
　　　　'Tis I; be not afraid."

From out the dazzling majesty,
Gently He'll lay His hand on thee,
Whispering: "Beloved, lov'st thou me?
'Twas not in vain I died for thee;
　　　　'Tis I; be not afraid."

Nature and Faith.

II Cor. 4 : 17, 18.

WE wept—'twas *Nature* wept, but Faith
Can pierce beyond the gloom of death,
And in yon world so fair and bright
Behold thee in refulgent light!
We miss thee here, yet *Faith* would rather
Know thou art with thy heavenly Father.
  Nature sees the body dead—
  Faith beholds the spirit fled;
  Nature stops at Jordan's tide—
  Faith beholds the other side;
  That but hears farewell and sighs,
  This, thy welcome in the skies;

  Nature mourns a *cruel* blow—
  Faith assures it is not so;
  Nature never sees thee more—
  Faith but sees thee gone before;
  Nature tells a dismal story—
  Faith has visions full of glory;
  Nature views the change with sadness—
  Faith contemplates it with gladness;

Nature murmurs—*Faith* gives meekness,
"Strength is perfected in weakness;"
Nature writhes, and hates the rod—
Faith looks up and blesses God;
Sense looks downwards—*Faith* above;
That sees harshness—*this* sees love.
Oh! let *Faith* victorious be—
Let it reign triumphantly!

But thou art gone! not lost, but flown,
Shall I then ask thee back, my own?
Back—and leave thy spirit's brightness?
Back—and leave thy robes of whiteness?
Back—and leave thine angel mould?
Back—and leave those streets of gold?
Back—and leave the Lamb who feeds thee?
Back—from founts to which He leads thee?
Back—and leave thy Heavenly Father?
Back—to earth and sin?—Nay rather
Would I live in solitude!
I *would* not ask thee if I *could;*
But patient wait the high decree,
That calls my spirit home to thee!

The Call.

THY night is dark; behold, the shade was deeper
    In the old garden of Gethsemane,
When that calm voice awoke the weary sleeper:
    "Couldst thou not watch one hour alone with me?"

O thou, so weary of thy self-denials!
    And so impatient of thy little cross,
Is it so hard to bear thy daily trials,
    To count all earthly things a gainful loss?

What if thou *always* suffer tribulation,
    And if thy Christian warfare never cease;
The gaining of the quiet habitation
    Shall gather thee to everlasting peace.

But here we all must suffer, walking lonely
    The path that Jesus once himself hath gone:
Watch thou in patience through the dark hour only,
    This one dark hour—before the eternal dawn.

The captive's oar may pause upon the galley,
  The soldier sleep beneath his pluméd crest,
And Peace may fold her wing o'er hill and valley,
  But thou, O Christian! must not take thy rest.

Thou must walk on, however man upbraid thee,
  With Him who trod the wine-press all alone;
Thou wilt not find one human hand to aid thee,
  One human soul to comprehend thine own.

Heed not the images forever thronging
  From out the foregone life thou liv'st no more;
Faint-hearted mariner! still art thou longing
  For the dim line of the receding shore.

Wilt thou find rest of soul in thy returning
  To that old path thou hast so vainly trod?
Hast thou forgotten all thy weary yearing
  To walk among the children of thy God?

Faithful and steadfast in their consecration,
  Living by that high faith to thee so dim,
Declaring before God their dedication,
  So far from thee because so near to him?

Canst thou forget thy Christian superscription,
  "Behold, we count them happy which endure?"
What treasure wouldst thou, in the land Egyptian,
  Repass the stormy water to secure?

And wilt thou yield thy sure and glorious promise
  For the poor fleeting joys earth can afford?
No hand can take away the treasure from us
  That rests within the keeping of the Lord.

Poor, wandering soul! I know that thou art seeking
  Some easier way, as all have sought before,
To silence the reproachful inward speaking—
  Some landward path unto an island shore.

The cross is heavy in thy human measure;
    The way too narrow for thine inward
        pride;
Thou canst not lay thine intellectual treasure
    At the low footstool of the Crucified.

Oh! that thy faithless soul, one great hour
        only,
    Would comprehend the Christian's perfect
        life;
Despised with Jesus, sorrowful and lonely,
    Yet calmly looking upward in its strife.

For poverty and self-renunciation,
    The Father yieldeth back a thousand-fold;
In the calm stillness of regeneration
    Cometh a joy we never knew of old.

In meek obedience to the heavenly Teacher,
    Thy weary soul can find its only peace;
Seeking no aid from any human creature—
    Looking to God alone for his release.

And he will come in his own time and power
    To set his earnest-hearted children free:
Watch only through this dark and painful
        hour,
    And the bright morning yet will break for
        thee.

God's Anvil.

PAIN'S furnace-heat within me quivers,
   God's breath upon the fire doth blow,
And all my heart in anguish shivers,
   And trembles at the fiery glow;
And yet I whisper, "As God will!"
And in his hottest fire hold still.

He comes, and lays my heart all heated
   On the bare anvil, minded so
Into his own fair shape to beat it
   With his great hammer, blow on blow;
And yet I whisper, "As God will!"
And at his heaviest blows hold still.

He takes my softened heart and beats it;
   The sparks fly off at every blow;
He turns it o'er and o'er, and heats it,
   And lets it cool, and makes it glow.
And yet I whisper, "As God will!"
And in his mighty hand hold still.

Why should I murmur? for the sorrow
   Thus only long-lived would be;
Its end may come, and will to-morrow,
   When God has done his work in me.
So I say trusting, "As God will!"
And trusting to the end, hold still.

He kindles for my profit purely,
   Affliction's glowing, fiery brand;
And all his heaviest blows are surely
   Inflicted by a master-hand.
So I say praying, "As God will!"
And hope in him and suffer still.

Means and Ends.

WE till to sow, we sow to reap,
We reap and grind it by and by:
We grind to bake, we bake to eat,
We eat to live, we live to die.
We die with Christ to rest in joy
In heaven, made free from all annoy.

The Cross and Crown.

MUST Jesus bear the cross alone,
   And all the world go free?
No; there's a cross for everyone;
   And there's a cross for me.

How happy are the saints above,
   Who once went sorrowing here;
But now they taste unmingled love
   And joy without a tear.

The consecrated cross I'll bear,
   Till death shall set me free;
And then go home my crown to wear,
   For there's a crown for me.

Upon the crystal pavement down,
   At Jesus' piercéd feet,
Joyful I'll cast my golden crown,
   And his dear name repeat.

And palms shall wave and harps shall ring
   Beneath heaven's arches high;
The Lord that lives, the ransomed sing,
   That lives no more to die.

Oh! My Saviour Crucified.

OH! my Saviour crucified,
Near thy cross may I abide;
There to gaze with steadfast eye
On thy dying agony.

Jesus, bruised and put to shame,
Tells me all the Father's name;
God is love, I surely know,
By my Saviour's depths of woe!

In his sinless soul's distress,
I behold my guiltiness;
Oh! how vile my low estate
Since my ransom was so great.

Dwelling on Mount Calvary,
Contrite shall my spirit be,
Rest and holiness shall find;
Fashioned like my Saviour's mind.

Even Me.

LORD! I hear of showers of blessing
  Thou art scattering full and free,
Showers the thirsty soul refreshing—
  Let some droppings fall on me,
            Even me.

Pass me not, O gracious Father!
  Lost and sinful though I be;
Thou mightst curse me, but the rather
  Let thy mercy light on me,
            Even me.

Pass me not, O tender Saviour!
  Let me love and cling to thee;
I am longing for thy favor;
  When thou comest, call for me,
            Even me.

Pass me not, O mighty Spirit!
  Thou canst make the blind to see;
Testify of Jesus' merit,
  Speak the word of peace to me,
            Even me.

Have I long in sin been sleeping,
  Long been slighting, grieving thee?
Has the world my heart been keeping?
  Oh! forgive and rescue me.
                    Even me.

Love of God! so pure and changeless;
  Blood of God! so rich and free;
Grace of God! so strong and boundless,
  Magnify it all in me,
                    Even me.

Pass me not, almighty Spirit!
  Draw this lifeless heart to thee;
Impute to me the Saviour's merit,
  Blessing others, oh! bless me.
                    Even me.

The Peace of God.

WE ask for peace, O Lord!
   Thy children ask thy peace;
Not what the world calls rest,
   That toil and care should cease;
That through bright sunny hours,
   Calm life should fleet away,
And tranquil night should fade
      In smiling day;
It is not for such peace that we would pray.

We ask for peace, O Lord!
   Yet not to stand secure,
Girt round with iron pride,
   Contented to endure;
Crushing the gentle strings
   That human hearts should know;
Untouched by others' joys
      Or others' woe.
Thou, O dear Lord! wilt never teach us so.

We ask thy peace, O Lord!
   Through storm and fear and strife.

To light and guide us on,
  Through a long, struggling life;
While no success or gain
  Shall cheer the desperate fight,
Or nerve what the world calls
    Our wasted might,
Yet pressing through the darkness to the light.

It is thine own, O Lord!
  Who toil while others sleep;
Who sow with living care
  What other hands shall reap;
They lean on thee entranced
  In calm and perfect rest;
Give us that peace, O Lord!
    Divine and blest,
Thou keepest for those hearts that love thee best.

Peace.

LIFE'S mystery, deep, restless as the ocean,
   Hath surged and wailed for ages to and fro;
Earth's generations watch its ceaseless motion,
   As in and out its hollow moanings flow.
Shivering and yearning by that unknown sea,
Let my soul calm itself, O God! in thee.

Life's sorrows, with inexorable power,
   Sweep desolation o'er this mortal plain;
And human loves and hopes fly as the chaff,
   Borne by the whirlwind, from the ripened grain.
Oh! when before that blast my hopes all flee,
Let my soul calm itself, O Christ! in thee.

Between the mysteries of death and life
   Thou standest, loving, guiding, not explaining;

We ask, and thou art silent; yet we gaze,
  And our charmed hearts forget their drear
    complaining.
No crushing fate, no stony destiny,
Thou " Lamb that hath been slain," we rest
  in thee.

The many waves of thought, the mighty
    tides,
  The ground-swell that rolls up from other
    lands,
From far-off worlds, from dim, eternal
    shores,
  Whose echo dashes o'er life's wave-worn
    strands;
This vague, dark tumult of the inner sea
Grows calm, grows bright, O risen Lord! in
  thee.

Thy piercéd hand guides the mysterious
    wheels,
  Thy thorn-crowned brow now wears the
    crown of power,
And when the dark enigma presseth sore,
  Thy patient voice saith : " Watch with me
    one hour."
As sinks the moaning river in the sea,
In silent peace, so sinks my soul in thee.

Prayer for Strength.

FATHER! before thy footstool kneeling,
   Once more my heart goes up to thee
For aid, for strength to thee appealing;
   Thou who alone canst succor me.

Hear me, for heart and flesh are failing,
   My spirit yielding in the strife;
And anguish, wild as unavailing,
   Sweeps in a flood across my life.

Help me to stem the tide of sorrow;
   Help me to bear thy chastening rod;
Give me endurance; let me borrow
   Strength from thy promise, O my God.

Not mine the grief which words may lighten;
   Not mine the tears of common woe;
The pang with which my heartstrings tighten,
   Only the all-seeing One may know.

And I am weak; my feeble spirit
   Shrinks from life's task in wild dismay;
Yet not that thou that task wouldst spare it,
   My Father, do I dare to pray.

Into my soul thy might infusing,
　　Strengthening my spirit by thine own,
Help me—all other aid refusing—
　　To cling to thee and thee alone.

And oh! in my exceeding weakness,
　　Make thy strength perfect — thou art strong—
Aid me to do thy will with meekness,
　　Thou, to whom all my powers belong.

Saviour! our human form once wearing,
　　Help, by the memory of that day,
When, painfully thy dark cross bearing,
　　E'en for a time thy strength gave way.

Beneath a lighter burden sinking,
　　Jesus, I cast myself on thee;
Forgive, forgive this useless shrinking
　　From trials that I know must be.

Oh! let me feel that thou art near me,
　　Close to thy side I shall not fear;
Hear me, O Strength of Israel! hear me;
　　Sustain and aid! in mercy, hear!

Onward.

TRAVELLER, faint not on the road,
    Droop not in the parching sun;
Onward, onward with thy load,
    Till the night be won;
Swerve not, though thy bleeding feet
    Fain the narrow path would leave,
From the burden and the heat;
    Thou shalt rest at eve.

Midst a world that round thee fades,
    Brightening stars and twilight life;
When a sacred calm pervades
    All that now is strife;
Rich the joy to be revealed
    In that hour from labor free,
Bright the splendors that shall yield
    Happiness to thee.

Master of a holy charm,
    Yet be patient on thy way;
Use the spell, and check the harm
    That would lead astray;

From the petty cares that teem,
   Turn thee, with prophetic eye,
To the glory of that dream
   Which shall never die.

By the mystery of thy trust;
   By the grandeur of that hour
When mortality and dust
   Clothed eternal power;
By the purple robe of shame,
   The mockery and the insulting rod;
By the anguish that o'ercame
   The incarnate God!

Faint not! fail not! be thou strong;
   Cast away distrust and fear,
Though the weary day seems long,
   Yet the night is near;
Friends and kindred wait beyond
   They who passed the trial pure;
Traveller, by that holy bond,
   Shrink not to endure.

For the New Year.

ANOTHER year, another year
   Has borne its record to the skies;
Another year, another year,
   Untried, unproved before us lies;
We hail with smiles its dawning ray—
How shall we meet its final day?

Another year, another year!
   Its squandered hours will ne'er return;
Oh! many a heart must quail with fear,
   O'er memory's blotted page to turn.
No record from that leaf will fade,
Not one erasure may be made.

Another year, another year!
   How many a grief has marked its flight!
Some whom we love no more are here—
   Translated to the realms of light.
Ah! none can bless the coming year
Like those no more to greet us here.

Another year, another year!
   Oh! many a blessing too was given,

Our lives to deck, our hearts to cheer,
    And antedate the joys of heaven;
But they too slumber in the past,
Where joys and griefs must sink at last.

Another year, another year!
    Gaze we no longer on the past,
Nor let us shrink with faithless fear
    From the dark shade the future casts.
The past, the future, what are they
To those whose lives may end to-day?

Another year, another year!
    Perchance the last of life below;
Who, ere its close, death's call may hear,
    None but the Lord of life can know.
Oh! to be found whene'er that day
May come, prepared to pass away.

Another year, another year!
    Help us earth's thorny path to tread;
So may each moment bring us near
    To thee, ere yet our lives are fled.
Saviour! we yield ourselves to thee,
For time and for eternity.

Dies Iræ.

(Translation of William J. Irons.)

DAY of wrath! O day of mourning!
See! once more the Cross returning,
Heaven and earth in ashes burning!

Oh what fear man's bosom rendeth
When from Heaven the Judge descendeth,
On whose sentence all dependeth!

Wondrous sound the Trumpet flingeth,
Through earth's sepulchres it ringeth,
All before the throne it bringeth!

Death is struck, and Nature quaking,
All creation is awaking,
To its Judge an answer making!

Lo! the Book, exactly worded,
Wherein all hath been recorded;
Thence shall judgment be awarded.

When the Judge His seat attaineth,
And each hidden deed arraigneth,
Nothing unavenged remaineth.

What shall I, frail man, be pleading,
Who for me be interceding,
When the just are mercy needing?

King of Majesty tremendous,
Who dost free salvation send us,
Fount of pity! then befriend us!

Think! kind Jesus, my salvation
Caused Thy wondrous incarnation;
Leave me not to reprobation!

Faint and weary Thou hast sought me,
On the Cross of suffering bought me,
Shall such grace be vainly brought me?

Righteous Judge of retribution,
Grant Thy gift of absolution,
Ere that reck'ning day's conclusion!

Guilty, now I pour my moaning,
All my shame with anguish owning;
Spare, O God, Thy suppliant groaning!

Thou the sinful woman savedst,
Thou the dying thief forgavest,
And to me a hope vouchsafest!

Worthless are my prayers and sighing,
Yet, good Lord, in grace complying,
Rescue me from fires undying!

With Thy favor'd sheep, oh place me!
Nor among the goats abase me;
But to Thy right hand upraise me.

While the wicked are confounded,
Doom'd to flames of woe unbounded,
Call me! with Thy saints surrounded.

Low I kneel with heart submission;
See, like ashes, my contrition;
Help me, in my last condition!

Ah! that Day of tears and mourning!
From the dust of earth returning,
Man for judgment must prepare him;
Spare, O God, in mercy spare him!

Lord, who didst our souls redeem,
Grant a blessed Requiem! Amen.

I Would Not Live Alway.

I WOULD not live alway—live alway below!
Oh no, I'll not linger, when bidden to go.
The days of our pilgrimage granted us here
Are enough for life's woes, full enough for its cheer.
Would I shrink from the path which the prophets of God,
Apostles, and Martyrs so joyfully trod?
While brethren and friends are all hastening home,
Like a spirit unblest, o'er the earth would I roam?

I would not live alway: I ask not to stay
Where storm after storm rises dark o'er the way;
Where, seeking for rest, I but hover around
Like the patriarch's bird, and no resting is found;
Where Hope, when she paints her gay bow in the air,

Leaves her brilliance to fade in the night of despair,
And Joy's fleeting angel ne'er sheds a glad ray,
Save the gleam of the plumage that bears him away.

I would not live alway, thus fetter'd by sin,
Temptation without, and corruption within;
In a moment of strength, if I sever the chain,
Scarce the victory is mine ere I'm captive again.
E'en the rapture of pardon is mingled with fears,
And the cup of thanksgiving with penitent tears.
The festival trump calls for jubilant songs,
But my spirit her own MISERERE prolongs.

I would not live alway: no, welcome the tomb;
Immortality's lamp burns there bright 'mid the gloom.
There, too, is the pillow where Christ bow'd his head;
Oh, soft be my slumbers on that holy bed!

And then the glad morn soon to follow that night,
When the sunrise of glory shall burst on my sight,
And the full matin-song as the sleepers arise
To shout in the morning, shall peal through the skies.

Who would like to live alway, away from his God,
Away from yon heaven, that blissful abode,
Where the rivers of pleasure flow o'er the bright plains,
And the noontide of glory eternally reigns;
Where the saints of all ages in harmony meet,
Their Saviour and brethren transported to greet,
While the anthems of rapture unceasingly roll,
And the smile of the Lord is the feast of the soul?

That heavenly music! what is it I hear?
The notes of the harpers ring sweet on my ear!
And see soft unfolding those portals of gold,
The King all array'd in His beauty behold.

Oh give me, Oh give me the wings of a dove!
Let me hasten my flight to those mansions
above:
Ay! 'tis now that my soul on swift pinions
would soar,
In ecstasy bid earth adieu evermore.

Grief was Sent Thee for Thy Good.

SOME there are who seem exempted
   From the doom incurred by all;
Are they not more sorely tempted?
   Are they not the first to fall?
As a mother's firm denial
   Checks her infant's wayward mood,
Wisdom lurks in every trial—
   Grief was sent thee for thy good.

In the scenes of former pleasure,
   Present anguish hast thou felt;
O'er thy fond heart's dearest treasure
   As a mourner hast thou knelt;
In thy hour of deep affliction,
   Let no impious thoughts intrude;
Meekly bow, with this conviction,
   Grief was sent thee for thy good.

Guide Me, O Thou Great Jehovah!

GUIDE me, O Thou great Jehovah!
   Pilgrim through this barren land;
I am weak, but Thou art mighty,
   Hold me with Thy powerful hand.
      Bread of Heaven! Bread of Heaven!
Feed me now and evermore!

Open now the crystal fountain,
   Whence the healing streams do flow;
Let the fiery cloudy pillar
   Lead me all my journey through;
      Strong Deliverer! Strong Deliverer!
Be Thou still my Strength and Shield!

When I tread the verge of Jordan,
   Bid my anxious fears subside;
Death of deaths, and hell's destruction,
   Land me safe on Canaan's side;
      Songs of praises, songs of praises,
I will ever give to Thee!

Musing on my habitation,
   Musing on my heavenly home,
Fills my soul with holy longing;
   Come, my Jesus, quickly come.
      Vanity is all I see;
      Lord, I long to be with Thee!

Just as I Am.

JUST as I am, without one plea
But that Thy Blood was shed for me,
And that Thou bidd'st me come to Thee,
    O Lamb of God, I come!

Just as I am, and waiting not
To rid my soul of one dark blot,
To Thee, whose Blood can cleanse each spot,
    O Lamb of God, I come!

Just as I am, though toss'd about
With many a conflict, many a doubt,
Fightings and fears within, without,
    O Lamb of God, I come!

Just as I am, poor, wretched, blind,
Sight, riches, healing of the mind,
Yea, all I need, in Thee to find,
    O Lamb of God, I come!

Just as I am, Thou wilt receive,
Wilt welcome, pardon, cleanse, relieve!
Because Thy promise I believe,
    O Lamb of God, I come!

Just as I am (Thy Love unknown
Has broken every barrier down),
Now, to be Thine, yea, Thine alone,
    O Lamb of God, I come!

Just as I am, of that free love
The breadth, length, depth, and height to
    prove,
Here for a season, then above,
    O Lamb of God, I come!

Oh! Had I Jubal's Lyre.

Oh! had I Jubal's lyre,
  Or Miriam's tuneful voice!
To sounds like his I would aspire,
  In songs like hers rejoice:
My humble strains but faintly show
  How much to Heaven and thee I owe.

Thy Will be Done.

MY God and Father, while I stray
Far from my home, on life's rough way,
Oh teach me from my heart to say,
    Thy will be done!

Though dark my path and sad my lot,
Let me be still and murmur not,
Or breathe the prayer divinely taught,
    Thy will be done!

What though in lonely grief I sigh
For friends beloved, no longer nigh,
Submissive still would I reply,
    Thy will be done!

Though Thou hast call'd me to resign
What most I prized, it ne'er was mine;
I have but yielded what was Thine;
    Thy will be done!

Should grief or sickness waste away
My life in premature decay,
My Father! still I strive to say
    Thy will be done!

Let but my fainting heart be blest
With Thy sweet Spirit for its guest,
My God, to Thee I leave the rest;
    Thy will be done!

Renew my will from day to day;
Blend it with Thine; and take away
All that now makes it hard to say
    Thy will be done!

Then, when on earth I breathe no more
The prayer, oft mix'd with tears before,
I'll sing, upon a happier shore,
    Thy will be done!

Nearer, My God, to Thee.

NEARER, my God, to Thee,
 Nearer to Thee!
E'en though it be a cross
 That raiseth me;
Still all my song shall be,
Nearer, my God, to Thee,
 Nearer to Thee!

Though like a wanderer,
 The sun gone down,
Darkness be over me,
 My rest a stone;
Yet in my dreams I'd be
Nearer, my God, to Thee,
 Nearer to Thee!

There let the way appear
 Steps into Heaven;
All that Thou send'st to me
 In mercy given;
Angels to beckon me
Nearer, my God, to Thee,
 Nearer to Thee!

Then with my waking thoughts
    Bright with Thy praise,
Out of my stony griefs
    Bethel I'll raise;
So by my woes to be
Nearer, my God, to Thee,
    Nearer to Thee!

Or if on joyful wing
    Cleaving the sky,
Sun, moon, and stars forgot,
    Upward I fly,
Still all my song shall be
Nearer, my God, to Thee,
    Nearer to Thee!

Abide With Me.

ABIDE with me! fast falls the even-tide;
The darkness deepens; Lord, with me abide!
When other helpers fail, and comforts flee,
Help of the helpless, oh abide with me!

Swift to its close ebbs out life's little day;
Earth's joys grow dim; its glories pass away;
Change and decay in all around I see:
O Thou, who changest not, abide with me!

Not a brief glance, I beg, a passing word:
But, as Thou dwell'st with Thy disciples, Lord,
Familiar, condescending, patient, free,
Come, not to sojourn, but abide, with me!

Come not in terrors, as the King of Kings;
But kind and good, with healing in Thy wings;
Tears for all woes, a heart for every plea;
Come, Friend of sinners, and thus 'bide with me!

Thou on my head in early youth didst smile;
And, though rebellious and perverse meanwhile,
Thou hast not left me, oft as I left Thee.
On to the close, O Lord, abide with me!

I need Thy Presence every passing hour;
What but Thy grace can foil the Tempter's power?
Who like Thyself my guide and stay can be?
Through cloud and sunshine, oh abide with me!

I fear no foe with Thee at hand to bless:
Ills have no weight, and tears no bitterness:
Where is Death's sting, where, Grave, thy victory?
I triumph still, if Thou abide with me!

Hold then Thy cross before my closing eyes!
Shine through the gloom, and point me to the skies!
Heaven's morning breaks, and earth's vain shadows flee;
In life and death, O Lord, abide with me!

Jesus, Lover of My Soul.

JESUS, lover of my soul,
   Let me to Thy bosom fly,
While the nearer waters roll,
   While the tempest still is high!
Hide me, O my Saviour, hide,
   Till the storm of life is past,
Safe into the haven guide;
   Oh, receive my soul at last!

Other refuge have I none!
   Hangs my helpless soul on Thee;
Leave, ah! leave me not alone,
   Still support and comfort me!
All my trust on Thee is stay'd,
   All my help from Thee I bring:
Cover my defenceless head
   With the shadow of Thy wing!

Wilt Thou not regard my call?
   Wilt Thou not accept my prayer?
Lo! I sink, I faint, I fall!
   Lo! on Thee I cast my care!

Reach me out Thy gracious hand!
  While I of Thy strength receive,
Hoping against hope I stand,
  Dying, and behold I live!

Thou, O Christ, art all I want;
  More than all in Thee I find:
Raise the fallen, cheer the faint,
  Heal the sick, and lead the blind;
Just and holy is Thy Name;
  I am all unrighteousness;
False and full of sin I am,
  Thou art full of truth and grace.

Plenteous grace with Thee is found—
  Grace to cover all my sin;
Let the healing streams abound;
  Make and keep me pure within!
Thou of Life the Fountain art;
  Freely let me take of Thee;
Spring Thou up within my heart!
  Rise to all Eternity!

Rock of Ages.

ROCK of Ages, cleft for me,
Let me hide myself in Thee;
Let the water and the blood,
From Thy riven side which flow'd,
Be of sin the double cure,
Cleanse me from its guilt and power.

Not the labors of my hands
Can fulfil Thy law's demands;
Could my zeal no respite know,
Could my tears forever flow,
All for sin could not atone;
Thou must save, and Thou alone.

Nothing in my hand I bring;
Simply to Thy Cross I cling;
Naked, come to Thee for dress;
Helpless, look to Thee for grace;
Foul, I to the Fountain fly;
Wash me, Saviour, or I die!

While I draw this fleeting breath,
When my eye-strings break in death,

When I soar through tracts unknown,
See Thee on Thy judgment-throne;
Rock of Ages, cleft for me,
Let me hide myself in Thee!

Angels, Roll the Rock Away!

ANGELS, roll the rock away;
Death, yield up the mighty prey!
See! the Saviour quits the tomb,
Glowing with immortal bloom.
    Hallelujah! hallelujah!
Christ the Lord is risen to-day.

Shout, ye seraphs! angels, raise
Your eternal song of praise!
Let the earth's remotest bound
Echo to the blissful sound!
    Hallelujah! hallelujah!
Christ the Lord is risen to-day.

Holy Father, holy Son,
Holy Spirit, Three in One,
Glory as of old to thee,
Now and evermore, shall be!
    Hallelujah! hallelujah!
Christ the Lord is risen to-day.

Coronation.

"ALL hail the power of Jesus' name!
    Let angels prostrate fall;
Bring forth the royal diadem,
    To crown Him Lord of all!

"Let high-born seraphs tune the lyre,
    And, as they tune it, fall
Before His face who tunes their choir,
    And crown Him Lord of all!

"Crown Him, ye morning stars of light
    Who fix'd this floating ball;
Now hail the Strength of Israel's might,
    And crown Him Lord of all!

"Crown Him, ye martyrs of your God,
    Who from His altar call;
Extol the stem of Jesse's rod,
    And crown Him Lord of all!

"Ye seed of Israel's chosen race,
    Ye ransom'd of the fall,
Hail Him who saves you by His grace,
    And crown Him Lord of all!

"Hail Him, ye heirs of David's line,
   Whom David Lord did call,
The God incarnate, man divine,
   And crown Him Lord of all!

"Sinners whose love can ne'er forget
   The wormwood and the gall,
Go spread your trophies at His feet,
   And crown Him Lord of all!

"Let every tribe and every tongue
   That bound creation's call
Now shout, in universal song,
   The crowned Lord of all!"

Death of a Christian.

CALM on the bosom of thy God,
   Fair spirit, rest thee now!
E'en while with ours thy footsteps trod,
   His seal was on thy brow.

Dust, to its narrow house beneath!
   Soul, to its place on high!
They that have seen thy look in death
   No more may fear to die.

My Faith Looks Up to Thee.

MY faith looks up to Thee,
Thou Lamb of Calvary,
   Saviour divine!
Now hear me while I pray:
Take all my guilt away;
Oh let me from this day
   Be wholly Thine!

May Thy rich grace impart
Strength to my fainting heart,
   My zeal inspire!
As thou hast died for me,
Oh may my love to Thee
Pure, warm, and changeless be,
   A living fire!

While life's dark maze I tread,
And griefs around me spread,
   Be thou my guide!
Bid darkness turn to day,
Wipe sorrow's tears away,
Nor let me ever stray
   From Thee aside.

When ends life's transient dream,
When death's cold, sullen stream
   Shall o'er me roll,
Blest Saviour! then in love
Fear and distrust remove;
Oh bear me safe above,
   A ransomed soul!

To a Child.

MY fairest child, I have no song to give you;
   No lark could pipe to skies so dull and gray;
Yet, ere we part, one lesson I can leave you
   For every day.

Be good, sweet maid, and let who will be clever;
   Do noble things—not dream them—all day long;
And so make life, death, and that vast forever
   One grand, sweet song.

When Our Heads are Bowed with Woe.

WHEN our heads are bow'd with woe,
When our bitter tears o'erflow,
When we mourn the lost, the dear,
Gracious Son of Mary, hear.

Thou our throbbing flesh hast worn,
Thou our mortal griefs hast borne,
Thou hast shed the human tear;
Gracious Son of Mary, hear.

When the sullen death-bell tolls
For our own departed souls,
When our final doom is near,
Gracious Son of Mary, hear.

Thou hast bow'd the dying head,
Thou the blood of life hast shed,
Thou hast fill'd a mortal bier;
Gracious Son of Mary, hear.

When the heart is sad within,
When the thought of all its sin,
When the spirit shrinks with fear,
Gracious Son of Mary, hear.

Thou the shame, the grief, hast known,
Though the sins were not Thine own;
Thou hast deign'd their load to bear;
Gracious Son of Mary, hear.

Jesus Only.

MATT. 17 : 8.

I.

"JESUS only!" In the shadow
  Of the cloud so chill and dim,
We are clinging, loving, trusting,
  He with us, and we with Him;
All unseen, though ever nigh,
"Jesus only"—all our cry,

II.

"Jesus only!" In the glory,
  When the shadows all are flow
Seeing Him in all His beauty,
  Satisfied with Him alone;
May we join His ransomed throng,
"Jesus only"—all our song!

Nothing but Leaves.

"He found nothing thereon but leaves."—MATT. xxi., 19.

NOTHING but leaves; the spirit grieves
    Over a wasted life;
Sin committed while conscience slept,
Promises made but never kept,
    Hatred, battle, and strife;
Nothing but leaves!

Nothing but leaves; no garner'd sheaves
    Of life's fair, ripen'd grain;
Words, idle words, for earnest deeds;
We sow our seeds—lo! tares and weeds;
    We reap with toil and pain
Nothing but leaves!

Nothing but leaves; memory weaves
    No veil to screen the past;
As we retrace our weary way,
Counting each lost and misspent day—
    We find, sadly, at last,
Nothing but leaves!

And shall we meet the Master so,
  Bearing our withered leaves?
The Saviour looks for perfect fruit—
We stand before him, humbled, mute;
  Waiting the words he breathes—
"*Nothing but leaves!*"

Truth.

"LIGHT after darkness, gain after loss,
  Strength after suffering, crown after cross.
  Sweet after bitter, song after sigh,
  Home after wandering, praise after cry.

"Sheaves after sowing, sun after rain,
  Sight after misery, peace after pain.
  Joy after sorrow, calm after blast,
  Rest after weariness, sweet rest at last.

"Near after distant, gleam after gloom,
  Love after loneliness, life after tomb.
  After long agony, rapture of bliss!
  Right was the pathway leading to this!"

Jesus! the Very Thought of Thee.

"Jesu, dulcis memoria."

JESUS! the very thought of Thee
   With sweetness fills my breast;
But sweeter far thy face to see,
   And in thy presence rest.

Nor voice can sing, nor heart can frame,
   Nor can the memory find
A sweeter sound than thy blest name,
   O Saviour of mankind!

O hope of every contrite heart,
   O joy of all the meek,
To those who fall, how kind thou art!
   How good to those who seek!

But what to those who find? ah! this
   Not tongue nor pen can show:
The love of Jesus, what it is,
   None but his loved ones know.

Jesus! our only joy be thou,
   As thou our prize will be;

Jesus! be thou our glory now,
  And through eternity.

O Jesus! King most wonderful!
  Thou Conqueror renowned!
Thou sweetness most ineffable,
  In whom all joys are found!

When once thou visitest the heart,
  Then truth begins to shine;
Then earthly vanities depart;
  Then kindles love divine.

O Jesus! light of all below!
  Thou fount of life and fire!
Surpassing all the joys we know,
  All that we can desire:

May every heart confess thy name,
  And ever thee adore;
And seeking thee, itself inflame
  To see thee more and more.

Thee may our tongues forever bless,
  Thee may we join above;
And ever in our lives express
  The image of thy love.

O Jesus! thou the beauty art
　　Of angel worlds above;
Thy name is music to the heart,
　　Enchanting it with love.

Celestial sweetness unalloyed!
　　Who eat thee hunger still;
Who drink of thee still feel a void,
　　Which naught but thou can fill.

O my sweet Jesus! hear the sighs
　　Which unto thee I send;
To thee mine inmost spirit cries,
　　My being's hope and end!

Stay with us, Lord, and with thy light
　　Illume the soul's abyss;
Scatter the darkness of our night,
　　And fill the world with bliss.

O Jesus! spotless Virgin flower!
　　Our life and joy! to thee
Be praise, beatitude, and power,
　　Through all eternity!

Christ.

Jesus, my Saviour, look on me,
For I am weary and opprest:
I come to cast my soul on thee,
      Thou art my *Rest*.

Look down on me, for I am weak;
I feel the toilsome journey's length;
Thine aid omnipotent I seek;
      Thou art my *Strength*.

I am bewildered on my way;
Dark and tempestuous is the night;
Oh, shed thou forth some cheering ray;
      Thou art my *Light*.

Why feel I desolate and lone?
Thy praises should my thoughts employ;
Thy presence can pour gladness down;
      Thou art my *Joy*.

Thou hast on me so much bestowed,
Surely I may relinquish health;
Thou'st made me rich, yea, rich towards
      God;
      Thou art my *Wealth*.

I hear the storms around me rise,
But when I dread the impending shock,
My spirit to her refuge flies;
      Thou art my *Rock*.

When the accuser flings his darts,
I look to thee—my terrors cease;
Thy cross a hiding-place imparts;
      Thou art my *Peace*.

Vain is all human help for me;
I dare not trust an earthly prop;
My sole reliance is on thee;
      Thou art my *Hope*.

Full many a conflict must be fought!
But shall I perish? shall I yield?
Is that bright motto given for naught?
      Thou art my *Shield*.

Standing alone on Jordan's brink,
In that tremendous, latest strife,
Thou wilt not suffer me to sink;
      Thou art my *Life*.

Thou wilt my every want supply
E'en to the end, whate'er befall;
Through life in death, eternally
      Thou art *my All*.

Stabat Mater.

"Stabat Mater Dolorosa."

"There stood by the cross of Jesus his mother."—John 19:25.

WEEPING stood his mother, sighing
By the cross where Jesus, dying,
    Hung aloft on Calvary:
Through her soul, in sorrow moaning,
Bowed in grief, in spirit groaning,
    Pierced the sword in misery.

Filled with grief beyond all others,
Mother—blessed among mothers—
    Of the God-begotten One!
How she sorroweth and grieveth,
Trembling as she thus perceiveth
    Dying her unspotted One!

Who could there refrain from weeping,
Seeing Christ's dear mother keeping
    In her grief so bitterly?
Who could fail to share her anguish,
Seeing thus the mother languish,
    Lost in woe so utterly?

For the trespass of his nation
She beheld his laceration,
    By their scourges suffering.
She beheld her dearest taken,
Crucified and God-forsaken,
    Dying by their torturing.

Mother, fountain of affection,
Let me share thy deep dejection,
    Let me share thy tenderness;
Let my heart, thy sorrow feeling
Love of Christ, the Lord revealing,
    Be like thine in holiness!

All his stripes, oh, let me feel them!
On my heart forever seal them,
    Printed there enduringly.
All his woes beyond comparing,
For my sake in anguish bearing,
    Let me share them willingly.

By thy side let me be weeping,
True condolence with him keeping,
    Weeping all my life with thee.
Near the cross with thee abiding,
Freely all thy woes dividing,
    In thy sorrow joined with thee.

Virgin of all virgins fairest,
Let me share the love thou bearest,
    Sharing all thy suffering:
Let me feel the death they gave him,
Crucified in shame to save them,
    Dying without murmuring.

Let me feel their blows so crushing,
Let me drink the current gushing
    From his wounds when crucified.
By a heavenly zeal excited,
When the judgment fires are lighted,
    Then may I be justified.

On the cross of Christ relying,
Through his death redeemed from dying,
    By his favor fortified;
When my mortal frame is perished,
Let my spirit then be cherished,
    And in Heaven be glorified.

The Shadow of the Rock.

THE Shadow of the Rock!
  Stay, pilgrim, stay!
Night treads upon the heels of day!
There is no other resting-place this way.
  The Rock is near,
  The well is clear;
Rest in the Shadow of the Rock!

The Shadow of the Rock!
  The desert wide
Lies round thee like a trackless tide,
In waves of sand forlornly multiplied.
  The sun is gone,
  Thou art alone;
Rest in the Shadow of the Rock!

The Shadow of the Rock!
  All come alone;
All, ever since the sun hath shone,
Who travelled by this road have come alone.
  Be of good cheer,
  A home is here;
Rest in the Shadow of the Rock!

The Shadow of the Rock!
Night veils the land;
How the palms whisper as they stand!
How the well tinkles faintly through the
    sand!
Cool water take
Thy thirst to slake;
Rest in the Shadow of the Rock!

The Shadow of the Rock!
Abide! abide!
This Rock moves ever at thy side,
Pausing to welcome thee at eventide.
Ages are laid
Beneath its shade;
Rest in the Shadow of the Rock!

The Shadow of the Rock!
Always at hand,
Unseen it cools the noontide land,
And quells the fire that flickers in the sand.
It comes in sight
Only at night;
Rest in the Shadow of the Rock!

The Shadow of the Rock!
Mid skies storm-riven
It gathers shadows out of heaven,

And holds them o'er us all night cool and
    even.
    Through the charmed air
    Dew falls not there;
Rest in the Shadow of the Rock!

    The Shadow of the Rock!
    To angels' eyes
This Rock its shadow multiplies,
And at this hour in countless places lies.
    Our Rock, one shade,
    O'er thousands laid!
Rest in the Shadow of the Rock!

    The Shadow of the Rock!
    To weary feet,
That have been diligent and fleet,
The sleep is deeper and the shade more
    sweet,
    O weary, rest!
    Thou art sore pressed;
Rest in the Shadow of the Rock!

    The Shadow of the Rock!
    Thy bed is made;
Crowds of tired souls like thine are laid
This night beneath the self-same placid
    shade.

    They who rest here
    Wake with Heaven near;
Rest in the Shadow of the Rock!

    The Shadow of the Rock!
      Pilgrim, sleep sound;
In night's swift hours with silent bound,
The Rock will put thee over leagues of
      ground,
    Gaining more way
    By night than day;
Rest in the Shadow of the Rock!

    The Shadow of the Rock!
      One day of pain,
Thou scarce wilt hope the Rock to gain,
Yet there wilt sleep thy last sleep on the
      plain,
    And only wake
    In Heaven's daybreak;
Rest in the Shadow of the Rock!

Jerusalem, the Golden.

JERUSALEM, the Golden!
   With milk and honey blest;
Beneath thy contemplation
   Sink heart and voice opprest.

I know not, oh! I know not
   What joys await us there;
What radiancy of glory,
   What bliss beyond compare.

They stand, those halls of Sion,
   All jubilant with song,
And bright with many an angel
   And all the martyr throng:

The Prince is ever in them,
   The daylight is serene;
The pastures of the blessed
   Are deck'd in glorious sheen.

There is the throne of David;
   And there, from care released,
The shout of them that triumph,
   The song of them that feast;

And they, who with their Leader
    Have conquer'd in the fight,
Forever and forever
    Are clad in robes of white.

Accepted.

ACCEPTED, Perfect, and Complete,
For God's inheritance made meet!
How true, how glorious, and how sweet!

In the Belovèd—by the King
Accepted, though not anything
But forfeit lives had we to bring.

And Perfect in Christ Jesus made,
On Him our great transgressions laid
We in His righteousnesss arrayed.

Complete in Him, our glorious Head,
With Jesus raisèd from the dead,
And by His mighty Spirit led!

O blessèd Lord, is this for me?
Then let my whole life henceforth be
One Alleluia-song to Thee!

Is This All?

SOMETIMES I catch sweet glimpses of His
    face,
    But that is all.
Sometimes He looks on me, and seems to
    smile,
    But that is all.
Sometimes He speaks a passing word of
    peace,
    But that is all.
Sometimes I think I hear His loving voice
    Upon me call.

And is this all He meant when thus He
    spoke—
    "Come unto me?"
Is there no deeper, more enduring rest,
    In Him for thee?
Is there no steadier light for thee in Him?
    Oh, come and see!

Oh, come and see! oh, look, and look again;
    All shall be right;
Oh, taste His love, and see that it is good,
    Thou child of night.

Oh, trust Him, trust Him in His grace and
    power;
  Then all is bright.

Nay, do not wrong Him by thy heavy
    thoughts,
  But love His love.
Do thou full justice to His tenderness,
    His mercy prove;
Take Him for what He is; oh, take Him all,
    And look above!

Then shall thy tossing soul find anchorage
    And steadfast peace;
Thy love shall rest on His; thy weary doubts
    Forever cease.
Thy heart shall find in Him, and in His
    grace,
  Its rest and bliss.

Christ and His love shall be thy blessed all
    For evermore!
Christ and His light shall shine on all thy
    ways
  For evermore!
Christ and His peace shall keep thy troubled
    soul
  For evermore!

"Thy Kingdom Come."

'TIS human lot to meet and bear
   The common ills of human life;
There's not a breast but hath its share
   Of bitter pain and vexing strife.
The peasant in his lowly shed,
   The noble 'neath a gilded dome,
Each will at some time bow his head,
   And ask and hope, "Thy Kingdom come!"

When some deep sorrow, surely slow,
   Despoils the cheek and eats the heart,
Laying our busy projects low,
   And bidding all earth's dreams depart—
Do we not smile, and calmly turn
   From the wide world's tumultuous hum,
And feel the immortal essence yearn,
   Rich with the thought, "Thy Kingdom come?"

The waves of Care may darkly bound
   And buffet, till, our strength outworn,
We stagger as they gather round,
   All shatter'd, weak, and tempest-torn;

But there's a lighthouse for the soul
   That beacons to a stormless home;
It safely guides through roughest tides—
   It shines, it saves! "Thy Kingdom come!"

To gaze upon the loved in death,
   To mark the closing, beamless eye,
To press dear lips and find no breath—
   This, this is life's worst agony!
But God, too merciful, too wise
   To leave the lorn one in despair,
Whispers, while snatching those we prize,
   "My Kingdom come!—Ye'll meet them there!"

Lead, Kindly Light.

LEAD, kindly light, amid th' encircling
    gloom,
  Lead Thou me on;
The night is dark, and I am far from home,
    Lead Thou me on;
Keep Thou my feet; I do not to ask see
The distant scene; one step enough for me.

I was not ever thus, nor pray'd that Thou
    Shouldst lead me on;
I loved to choose and see my path; but now
    Lead Thou me on!
I loved the garish day, and, spite of fears,
Pride ruled my will. Remember not past
    years!

So long Thy power has blest me, sure it still
    Will lead me on
O'er moor and fen, o'er crag and torrent, till
    The night is gone,
And with the morn those angel faces smile
Which I have loved long since, and lost a
    while!

Jerusalem, My Happy Home.

JERUSALEM, my happy home!
   Name ever dear to me!
When shall my labors have an end,
   In joy, and peace, and thee?

When shall these eyes thy heaven-built walls
   And pearly gates behold;
Thy bulwarks with salvation strong,
   And streets of shining gold?

Oh when, thou city of my God,
   Shall I thy courts ascend;
Where congregations ne'er break up
   And Sabbaths have no end?

Apostles, martyrs, prophets, there
   Around my Saviour stand;
And soon my friends in Christ below
   Will join the glorious band.

JERUSALEM, my happy home!
   My soul still pants for thee;
Then shall my labors have an end,
   When I thy joys shall see.

Come to Me!

WITH tearful eyes I look around;
   Life seems a dark and stormy sea;
Yet midst the gloom I hear a sound,
   A heavenly whisper—Come to Me!

It tells me of a place of rest;
   It tells me where my soul may flee:
Oh! to the weary, faint, opprest,
   How sweet the bidding—Come to Me!

When the poor heart with anguish learns
   That earthly props resign'd must be,
And from each broken cistern turns,
   It hears the accents—Come to Me!

When against sin I strive in vain,
   And cannot from its yoke get free,
Sinking beneath the heavy chain,
   The words arrest me—Come to Me!

When nature shudders, loath to part
   From all I love, enjoy, and see;
When a faint chill steals o'er my heart,
   A sweet voice utters—Come to Me!

Come, for all else must fail and die;
    Earth is no resting-place for thee;
Heavenward direct thy weeping eye;
    I am thy Portion—Come to Me!

Oh, voice of mercy, voice of love!
    In conflict, grief, and agony,
Support me, cheer me from above,
    And gently whisper—Come to Me!

Easter.

JESUS Christ to-day is risen,
    And o'er death triumphant reigns;
He has burst the grave's strong prison,
    Leading Sin herself in chains.
                   Kyrie Eleison.

For our sins the sinless Saviour
    Bare the heavy wrath of God;
Reconciling us, that favor
    Might be shown us through his blood.
                     Kyrie Eleison.

In his hands he hath forever
    Mercy, life, and sin, and death;
Christ his people can deliver
    All who come to him in faith.
                     Kyrie Eleison.

Unrest.

HEART, weary heart! what means thy wild
    unrest?
  Hast thou not tasted of earth's every
    pleasure?
With all that mortals seek thy lot is blest;
  Yet dost thou ever chant in mournful
    measure—
        "Something beyond!"

Heart, weary heart! canst thou not find re-
    pose
  In the sweet calm of friendship's pure de-
    votion?
Amid the peace which sympathy bestows,
  Still dost thou murmur, with repress'd
    emotion,—
        "Something beyond!"

Heart, weary heart! too idly hast thou
    pour'd
Thy music and thy perfume on the blast!
Now, beggar'd in affection's treasured hoard,
  Thy cry is still—thy saddest and thy last—
        "Something beyond!"

Heart, weary heart! oh, cease thy wild un-
   rest!
Earth cannot satisfy thy bitter yearning,—
Then onward, upward speed thy lonely guest,
   And hope to find, where Heaven's pure
      stars are burning,
            " Something beyond!"

I Sought the Lord.

I SOUGHT the Lord—He heard my voice,
   The hour of my sorrow pass'd away;
He bade my trembling soul rejoice,
   And smooth'd the paths where now I
      stray:
I look back to the past where never
   My footsteps shall return again,
For, in *His* path I'll walk forever,
   And steadfast in my faith remain!

I sought the Lord—and me He heard,
   He let my prayers to Heaven ascend;
And trusting in His holy word,
   I knew no other hope or friend;
And now with meek and chasten'd spirit
   I pray my sins may be forgiven,
That I, hereafter, may inherit
   A rest above—a home in Heaven.

The Voice of Jesus.

I HEARD the voice of Jesus say,
  "Come unto me and rest;
Lay down, thou weary one, lay down
  Thy head upon my breast."
I came to Jesus as I was,
  Weary, and worn, and sad;
I found in Him a resting-place,
  And He has made me glad.

I heard the voice of Jesus say,
  "Behold! I freely give
Thee living water; thirsty one,
  Stoop down, and drink, and live!"
I came to Jesus, and I drank
  Of that life-giving stream;
My thirst was quench'd, my soul revived,
  And now I live in Him.

I heard the voice of Jesus say,
  "I am this dark world's light;
Look unto Me, thy morn shall rise,
  And all thy day be bright."
I look'd to Jesus, and I found
  In Him my star, my sun;
And in that light of life I'll walk
  Till travelling days are done.

"Master, Say On!"

MASTER, speak! Thy servant heareth,
   Waiting for Thy gracious word,
Longing for Thy voice that cheereth;
   Master! let it now be heard.
I am listening, Lord, for Thee;
What hast Thou to say to me?

Master, speak in love and power:
   Crown the mercies of the day,
In this quiet evening hour
   Of the moonrise o'er the bay,
With the music of Thy voice;
Speak! and bid Thy child rejoice.

Often through my heart is pealing
   Many another voice than Thine,
Many an unwilled echo stealing
   From the walls of this Thy shrine:
Let Thy longed-for accents fall;
Master, speak! and silence all.

Master, speak! I do not doubt Thee,
    Though so tearfully I plead;
Saviour, Shepherd! oh, without Thee
    Life would be a blank indeed!
But I long for fuller light,
Deeper love and clearer sight.

Resting on the "faithful saying,"
    Trusting what Thy Gospel saith,
On Thy written promise staying
    All my hope in life and death,
Yet I long for something more
From Thy love's exhaustless store.

Speak to me by name, O Master,
    Let me know it is to me;
Speak, that I may follow faster,
    With a step more firm and free,
Where the Shepherd leads the flock,
In the shadow of the Rock.

Master, speak! I kneel before Thee,
    Listening, longing, waiting still;
Oh, how long shall I implore Thee
    This petition to fulfil?
Hast Thou not one word for me?
Must my prayer unanswered be?

Master, speak! though least and lowest,
  Let me not unheard depart;
Master, speak! for oh, Thou knowest
  All the yearning of my heart,
Knowest all its truest need;
Speak! and make me blest indeed.

Master, speak! and make me ready,
  When Thy voice is truly heard,
With obedience glad and steady
  Still to follow every word.
I am listening, Lord, for Thee;
Master, speak, oh, speak to me!

The Ascension.

HE is gone—beyond the skies,
A cloud receives Him from our eyes;
Gone beyond the highest height
Of mortal's gaze or angel's flight;
Through the veils of time and space,
Pass'd into the holiest place;
All the toil, the sorrow done,
All the battle fought and won.

He is gone—and we return,
And our hearts within us burn;
Olivet no more shall greet,
With welcome shout, His coming feet;
Never shall we thank Him more
On Gennesareth's glist'ning shore,
Never in that look or voice
Shall Zion's walls again rejoice.

He is gone—and we remain
In this world of sin and pain,
In the void which He has left;
On this earth, of Him bereft;

We have still His work to do,
We can still His path pursue,
Seek Him both in friend or foe,
In ourselves His image show.

He is gone—but we once more
Shall behold Him as before,
In the Heaven of Heavens, the same
As on earth He went and came;
In the many mansions there,
Peace for us He will prepare;
In that world unseen, unknown,
He and we may yet be one.

He is gone—but not in vain;
Wait, until He comes again;
He is risen, He is not here,
Far above this earthly sphere;
Evermore in heart and mind
There our peace in Him we find,
To our own Eternal Friend,
Thitherward let us ascend.

"Amen!"

SO let it be! The prayer that Christ enjoins
Live ever in our soul and on our tongue!
So let it be! The worship he assigns,
Our great Creator, with thanksgiving song,
From hearths, in temples, yea, in woods among,
Pour forth! So let it be! As drooping vines
Drink the reviving shower, so sink along
Our hearts his precepts! Lo, one word enshrines
Full attestation of our faith! "Amen"
Includes the sum of our assent, and bears
The seal of truth: it is the wing of prayers,
Speeding the voice of millions, not in vain,
To God's high throne, borne on seraphic airs,
To ratify in heaven our glorious gain!

Sunday Morning Bells.

FROM the near city comes the clang of bells:
Three hundred jarring diverse tones combine
In one faint misty harmony, as fine
As the soft note yon winter robin swells.
What if to Thee in thine infinity
These multiform and many-colored creeds
Seem but the robe man wraps as masquers' weeds
Round the one living truth thou givest him—Thee?
What if these varied forms that worship prove,
Being heart-worship, reach thy perfect ear
But as a monotone, complete and clear,
Of which the music is, through Christ's name, love?
Forever rising in sublime increase
To "Glory in the highest,—on earth peace?"

The Master's Call.

RISE, said the Master, come unto the feast.
She heard the call, and rose with willing
  feet;
But thinking it not otherwise than meet
For such a bidding to put on her best,
She is gone from us for a few short hours
Into her bridal closet, there to wait
For the unfolding of the palace-gate
That gives her entrance to the blissful
  bowers.
We have not seen her yet, though we have
  been
Full often to her chamber-door, and oft
Have listened underneath the postern green,
And laid fresh flowers, and whispered short
  and soft;
But she hath made no answer; and the day
From the clear west is fading fast away.

Veni Creator Spiritus.

COME, Holy Ghost, our souls inspire,
And lighten with celestial fire;
Thou the anointing Spirit art,
Who dost Thy seven-fold gifts impart:
Thy blessed unction from above,
Is comfort, life, and fire of love;
Enable, with perpetual light,
The dulness of our blinded sight;
Anoint and cheer our soiled faced
With the abundance of Thy grace:
Keep far our foes, give peace at home;
Where Thou art Guide, no ill can come.
Teach us to know the Father, Son,
And Thee, of both, to be but one;
That, through the ages all along,
This may be our endless song;
  Praise to Thy eternal merit,
  Father, Son, and Holy Spirit.

The Ministry of Song.

IN God's great field of labor
    All work is not the same;
He hath a service for each one
    Who loves His holy name.
And you, to whom the secrets
    Of all sweet sounds are known,
Rise up! for He hath called you
    To a mission of your own.
And, rightly to fulfil it,
    His grace can make you strong,
Who to your charge hath given
    The Ministry of Song.

Sing to the little children,
    And they will listen well;
Sing grand and holy music,
    For they can feel its spell.
Tell them the tale of Jephthah;
    Then sing them what he said—
"Deeper and deeper still," and watch
    How the little cheek grows red,

And the little breath comes quicker:
   They will ne'er forget the tale,
Which the song has fastened surely,
   As with a golden nail.

I remember, late one evening,
   How the music stopped; for hark!
Charlie's nursery door was open,
   He was calling in the dark—
"Oh no! I am not frightened,
   And I do not want a light;
But I cannot sleep for thinking
   Of the song you sang last night.
Something about a 'valley,'
   And 'make rough places plain,'
And 'Comfort ye;' so beautiful!
   Oh, sing it me again!"

Sing at the cottage bedside;
   They have no music there,
And the voice of praise is silent
   After the voice of prayer.
Sing of the gentle Saviour
   In the simplest hymns you know,
And the pain-dimmed eye will brighten
   As the soothing verses flow.

Better than loudest plaudits
   The murmured thanks of such,
For the King will stoop to crown them
   With His gracious "Inasmuch."

Sing, where the full-toned organ
   Resounds through aisle and nave,
And the choral praise ascendeth
   In concord sweet and grave.
Sing, where the village voices
   Fall harshly on your ear;
And, while more earnestly you join,
   Less discord you will hear.
The noblest and the humblest
   Alike are "common praise,"
And not for human ear alone
   The psalm and hymn we raise.

Sing in the deepening twilight,
   When the shadow of eve is nigh,
And her purple and golden pinions
   Fold o'er the western sky.
Sing in the silver silence,
   While the first moonbeams fall;
So shall your power be greater
   Over the hearts of all.

Sing till you bear them with you
  Into a holy calm,
And the sacred tones have scattered
  Manna, and myrrh, and balm.

Sing! that your song may gladden;
  Sing like the happy rills,
Leaping in sparkling blessing
  Fresh from the breezy hills.
Sing! that your song may silence
  The folly and the jest,
And the "idle word" be banished
  As an unwelcome guest.
Sing! that your song may echo,
  After the strain is past,
A link of the love-wrought cable
  That holds some vessel fast.

Sing to the tired and anxious;
  It is yours to fling a ray,
Passing, indeed, but cheering,
  Across the rugged way.
Sing to God's holy servants,
  Weary with loving toil,
Spent with their faithful labor
  On oft ungrateful soil.

The chalice of your music
    All reverently bear,
For with the blessèd angels
    Such ministry you share.

When you long to bear the Message
    Home to some troubled breast,
Then sing with loving fervor,
    "Come unto Him, and rest."
Or would you whisper comfort,
    Where words bring no relief,
Sing how " He was despisèd,
    Acquainted with our grief,"
And, aided by His blessing,
    The song may win its way
Where speech had no admittance,
    And change the night to-day.

Sing, when His mighty mercies
    And marvellous love you feel,
And the deep joy of gratitude
    Springs freshly as you kneel;
When words, like morning starlight,
    Melt powerless, rise and sing!
And bring your sweetest music
    To Him, your gracious King.

Pour out your song before Him
    To whom our best is due;
Remember, He who hears your prayer
    Will hear your praises too.

Sing on in grateful gladness!
    Rejoice in this good thing
Which the Lord thy God hath given thee,
    The happy power to sing.
But yield to Him, the Sovereign,
    To whom all gifts belong,
In fullest consecration,
    Your Ministry of Song,
Until His mercy grant you
    That resurrection voice,
Whose only ministry shall be
    To praise Him and rejoice.

HENRY ALTEMUS' PUBLICATIONS.
PHILADELPHIA, PA.

THE RISE OF THE DUTCH REPUBLIC (a History). By John Lothrop Motley. A new and handsome library edition of a Grand Historical Work. Embellished with over 50 full-page half-tone Engravings. Complete in two volumes—over 1,600 pages. Crown 8vo. Cloth, per set, $2.00. Half Morocco, gilt top, per set, $3.25.

QUO VADIS. A tale of the time of Nero, by Henryk Sienkiewicz. Complete and unabridged. Translated by Dr. S. A. Binton, author of "Ancient Egypt," etc., and S. Malevsky, with illustrations by M. DeLipman. Crown 8vo. Cloth, ornamental, 515 pages, $1.25.

MANUAL OF MYTHOLOGY. For the use of Schools, Art Students, and General Readers, by Alexander S. Murray, Department of Greek and Roman Antiquities, British Museum. With Notes, Revisions, and Additions by William H. Klapp, Headmaster of the Protestant Episcopal Academy, Philadelphia. With 200 illustrations, and an exhaustive Index. Large 12mo., 450 pages, $1.25.

"It has been acknowledged the best work on the subject to be found in a concise form, and, as it embodies the results of the latest researches and discoveries in ancient mythologies, it is superior for school and general purposes as a hand book to any of the so-called standard works."

THE AGE OF FABLE: OR BEAUTIES OF MYTHOLOGY. By Thomas Bulfinch, with Notes. Revisions, and Additions by William H. Klapp, Headmaster of the Protestant Episcopal Academy, Philadelphia. With 200 illustrations and an exhaustive Index. Large 12mo., 450 pages, $1.25.

This work has always been regarded as classical authority.
"The Grecian mythology is so intimately connected with the work of the greatest poets that it will continue to be interesting as long as classical poetry exists, and must form an indispensable part of the education of the man of literature and of the gentleman.—*Edmund Burke.*

TAINE'S ENGLISH LITERATURE, translated from the French by Henry Van Laun, illustrated with 20 fine photogravure portraits. Best English library edition, four volumes, cloth, full gilt, octavo, per set, $10.00. Half calf, per set, $12.50. Cheaper edition, with frontispiece illustrations only, cloth, paper titles, per set, $7.50.

STEPHEN. A SOLDIER OF THE CROSS, by Florence Morse Kingsley, author of "Titus, a Comrade of the Cross." "Since Ben-Hur no story has so vividly portrayed the times of Christ."—*The Bookseller.* Cloth, 12mo., 369 pages. $1.25.

HENRY ALTEMUS' PUBLICATIONS.

BUNYAN'S PILGRIM'S PROGRESS, with 100 engravings by Frederick Barnard and others. Cloth, small quarto (9x10 inches), $1.00.

DICKENS' CHILD'S HISTORY OF ENGLAND, with 75 fine engravings by famous artists. Cloth, small quarto, boxed (9x10 inches), $1.00.

BIBLE PICTURES AND STORIES, 100 full page engravings. Cloth, small quarto (7x9 inches), $1.00.

MY ODD LITTLE FOLK, some rhymes and verses about them, by Malcolm Douglass. Numerous original engravings. Cloth, small quarto (7x9 inches), $1.00.

PAUL AND VIRGINIA, by Bernardin de St. Pierre, with 125 engravings by Maurice Leloir. Cloth, small quarto (9x10), $1.00.

LIFE AND ADVENTURES OF ROBINSON CRUSOE, with 120 original engravings by Walter Paget. Cloth, octavo (7½x9¾), $1.50.

ALTEMUS' ILLUSTRATED LIBRARY OF STANDARD AUTHORS.

Cloth, Twelve Mo. Size, 5½x7¾ Inches. Each $1.00.

TALES FROM SHAKESPEARE, by Charles and Mary Lamb, with 155 illustrations by famous artists.

PAUL AND VIRGINIA, by Bernardin de St. Pierre, with 125 engravings by Maurice Leloir.

ALICE'S ADVENTURES IN WONDERLAND, AND THROUGH THE LOOKING-GLASS AND WHAT ALICE FOUND THERE, by Lewis Carroll. Complete in one volume with 92 engravings by John Tenniel.

LUCILE, by Owen Meredith, with numerous illustrations by George Du Maurier, author of Trilby.

BLACK BEAUTY, by Anna Sewell, with nearly 50 original engravings.

SCARLET LETTER, by Nathaniel Hawthorne, with numerous original full-page and text illustrations.

THE HOUSE OF THE SEVEN GABLES, by Nathaniel Hawthorne, with numerous original full-page and text illustrations.

BATTLES OF THE WAR FOR INDEPENDENCE, by Prescott Holmes, with 70 illustrations.

BATTLES OF THE WAR FOR THE UNION, by Prescott Holmes, with 80 illustrations.

THE SONG OF HIAWATHA, by Henry W. Longfellow, with 100 illustrations.

HENRY ALTEMUS' PUBLICATIONS.

ALTEMUS' YOUNG PEOPLES' LIBRARY.
Price, 50 cents each.

ROBINSON CRUSOE: (Chiefly in words of one syllable). His life and strange, surprising adventures, with 70 beautiful illustrations by Walter Paget.

ALICE'S ADVENTURES IN WONDERLAND, with 42 illustrations by John Tenniel. "The most delightful of children's stories. Elegant and delicious nonsense."—*Saturday Review.*

THROUGH THE LOOKING-GLASS AND WHAT ALICE FOUND THERE; a companion to "Alice in Wonderland," with 50 illustrations by John Tenniel.

BUNYAN'S PILGRIM'S PROGRESS, with 50 full page and text illustrations.

A CHILD'S STORY OF THE BIBLE, with 72 full page illustrations.

A CHILD'S LIFE OF CHRIST, with 49 illustrations. God has implanted in the infant heart a desire to hear of Jesus, and children are early attracted and sweetly riveted by the wonderful Story of the Master from the Manger to the Throne.

SWISS FAMILY ROBINSON, with 50 illustrations. The father of the family tells the tale of the vicissitudes through which he and his wife and children pass, the wonderful discoveries made and dangers encountered. The book is full of interest and instruction.

CHRISTOPHER COLUMBUS AND THE DISCOVERY OF AMERICA, with 70 illustrations. Every American boy and girl should be acquainted with the story of the life of the great discoverer, with its struggles, adventures, and trials.

THE STORY OF EXPLORATION AND DISCOVERY IN AFRICA, with 80 illustrations. Records the experiences of adventures and discoveries in developing the "Dark Continent," from the early days of Bruce and Mungo Park down to Livingstone and Stanley, and the heroes of our own times. No present can be more acceptable than such a volume as this, where courage, intrepidity, resource, and devotion are so admirably mingled.

THE FABLES OF ÆSOP. Compiled from the best accepted sources: With 62 illustrations. The fables of Æsop are among the very earliest compositions of this kind, and probably have never been surpassed for point and brevity.

HENRY ALTEMUS' PUBLICATIONS.

Altemus' Young Peoples' Library—Continued.

Price, 50 cents each.

GULLIVER'S TRAVELS. Adapted for young readers, with 50 illustrations.

MOTHER GOOSE'S RHYMES, JINGLES AND FAIRY TALES, with 234 illustrations.

LIVES OF THE PRESIDENTS OF THE UNITED STATES, by Prescott Holmes. With portraits of the Presidents and also of the unsuccessful candidates for the office; as well as the ablest of the Cabinet officers. It is just the book for intelligent boys, and it will help to make them intelligent and patriotic citizens.

THE STORY OF ADVENTURE IN THE FROZEN SEAS, with 70 illustrations. By Prescott Holmes. We have here brought together the records of the attempts to reach the North Pole. The book shows how much can be accomplished by steady perseverance and indomitable pluck.

ILLUSTRATED NATURAL HISTORY, by the Rev. J. G. Wood, with 80 illustrations. This author has done more to popularize the study of natural history than any other writer. The illustrations are striking and life-like.

A CHILD'S HISTORY OF ENGLAND, by Charles Dickens, with 50 illustrations. Tired of listening to his children memorize the twaddle of old fashioned English history the author covered the ground in his own peculiar and happy style for his own children's use. When the work was published its success was instantaneous.

BLACK BEAUTY; THE AUTOBIOGRAPHY OF A HORSE, by Anna Sewell, with 50 illustrations. A work sure to educate boys and girls to treat with kindness all members of the animal kingdom. Recognized as the greatest story of animal life extant.

THE ARABIAN NIGHTS ENTERTAINMENTS, with 130 illustrations. Contains the most favorably known of the stories.

GRIMM'S FAIRY TALES. With 55 illustrations. The Tales are a wonderful collection, as interesting, from a literary point of view, as they are delightful as stories.

FLOWER FABLES. By Louisa May Alcott. With numerous illustrations, full page and text. A series of very interesting fairy tales by the most charming of American story-tellers.

HENRY ALTEMUS' PUBLICATIONS.

Altemus' Young Peoples' Library—Continued.
Price, 50 cents each.

ANDERSEN'S FAIRY TALES. By Hans Christian Andersen. With 77 illustrations.
The spirit of high moral teaching, and the delicacy of sentiment, feeling, and expression that pervade these tales make these wonderful creations not only attractive to the young, but equally acceptable to those of mature years, who are able to understand their real significance and appreciate the depth of their meaning.

GRANDFATHER'S CHAIR: A HISTORY FOR YOUTH. By Nathaniel Hawthorne. With 60 illustrations.
The story of America from the landing of the Puritans to the acknowledgment without reserve of the Independence of the United States, told with all the elegance, simplicity, grace, clearness, and force for which Hawthorne is conspicuously noted.

ALTEMUS' DEVOTIONAL SERIES.

Standard Religious Literature Appropriately Bound in Handy Volume Size. Each Volume contains Illuminated Title, Portrait of Author, and Appropriate Illustrations.

White Vellum, Gold and Monotints, Boxed, each 50 cents.

1. **KEPT FOR THE MASTER'S USE**, by Frances Ridley Havergal. "Will perpetuate her name."
2. **MY KING AND HIS SERVICE, OR DAILY THOUGHTS FOR THE KING'S CHILDREN**, by Frances Ridley Havergal. "Simple, tender, gentle, and full of Christian love."
3. **MY POINT OF VIEW.** Selections from the works of Professor Henry Drummond.
4. **OF THE IMITATION OF CHRIST**, by Thomas A'Kempis. "With the exception of the Bible it is probably the book most read in Christian literature."
5. **ADDRESSES**, by Professor Henry Drummond. "Intelligent sympathy with the Christian's need."

HENRY ALTEMUS' PUBLICATIONS.

Altemus' Devotional Series—Continued.
Price, 50 cents each.

6 NATURAL LAW IN THE SPIRITUAL WORLD, by Professor Henry Drummond. "A most notable book which has earned for the author a world-wide reputation."

7 ADDRESSES, by the Rt. Rev. Phillips Brooks. "Has exerted a marked influence over the rising generation."

8 ABIDE IN CHRIST. Thoughts on the Blessed Life of Fellowship with the Son of God. By the Rev. Andrew Murray. "It cannot fail to stimulate and cheer."—*Spurgeon.*

9 LIKE CHRIST. Thoughts on the Blessed Life of Conformity to the Son of God. By the Rev. Andrew Murray. A sequel to "Abide in Christ." "May be read with comfort and edification by all."

10 WITH CHRIST IN THE SCHOOL OF PRAYER, by the Rev. Andrew Murray. "The best work on prayer in the language."

11 HOLY IN CHRIST. Thoughts on the calling of God's Children to be Holy as He is Holy. By the Rev. Andrew Murray. "This sacred theme is treated Scripturally and robustly without spurious sentimentalism."

12 THE MANLINESS OF CHRIST, by Thomas Hughes, author of "Tom Brown's School Days," etc. "Evidences of the sublimest courage and manliness in the boyhood, ministry, and in the last acts of Christ's life."

13 ADDRESSES TO YOUNG MEN, by the Rev. Henry Ward Beecher. Seven addresses on common vices and their results.

14 THE PATHWAY OF SAFETY, by the Rt. Rev. Ashton Oxenden, D. D. Some words of advice and encouragement on the text "What Must I do to be Saved."

15 THE CHRISTIAN LIFE, by the Rt. Rev. Ashton Oxenden, D. D. A beautiful delineation of an ideal life from the conversion to the final reward.

16 THE THRONE OF GRACE. Before which the burdened soul may cast itself on the bosom of infinite love and enjoy in prayer "a peace which passeth all understanding."

HENRY ALTEMUS' PUBLICATIONS.

Altemus' Devotional Series—Continued.
Price, 50 cents each.

17 THE PATHWAY OF PROMISE, by the author of "The Throne of Grace." Thoughts consolatory and encouraging to the Christian pilgrim as he journeys onward to his heavenly home.

18 THE IMPREGNABLE ROCK OF HOLY SCRIPTURE, by the Rt. Hon. William Ewart Gladstone, M. P. The most masterly defence of the truths of the Bible extant. The author says: The Christian Faith and the Holy Scriptures arm us with the means of neutralizing the assaults of evil in and from ourselves.

19 STEPS INTO THE BLESSED LIFE, by the Rev. F. B. Meyer, B. A. A powerful help towards sanctification.

20 THE MESSAGE OF PEACE, by the Rev. Richard W. Church, D. D. Eight excellent sermons on the advent of the Babe of Bethlehem and his influence and effect on the world.

21 JOHN PLOUGHMAN'S TALK, by the Rev. Charles H. Spurgeon.

22 JOHN PLOUGHMAN'S PICTURES, by the Rev. Charles H. Spurgeon.

23 THE CHANGED CROSS; AND OTHER RELIGIOUS POEMS.

24 GOLD DUST. A collection of Golden Counsels for the Sanctification of Daily Life. Edited by Charlotte M. Yonge.

25 DAILY FOOD FOR CHRISTIANS. Being a Promise and another Scriptural portion for every day in the year; together with the Verse of a Hymn.

26 PEEP OF DAY. Or a Series of the Earliest Religious Instruction the Infant Mind is Capable of Receiving.

27 LINE UPON LINE. Or a second Series of the Earliest Religious Instruction the Infant Mind is Capable of Receiving.

28 PRECEPT UPON PRECEPT. By the author of "The Peep of Day," "Line Upon Line," "Precept Upon Precept," etc.

29 THE PRINCE OF THE HOUSE OF DAVID, by the Rev. J. H. Ingraham.

30 JESSICA'S FIRST PRAYER AND JESSICA'S MOTHER, by Hesba Stretton.

HENRY ALTEMUS' PUBLICATIONS.

ALTEMUS' NEW ILLUSTRATED VADEMECUM SERIES.

Masterpieces of English and American Literature, Handy Volume Size, Large Type Editions. Each Volume Contains Illuminated Title Pages, and Portrait of Author and Numerous Engravings.

Full cloth, ivory finish, ornamental inlaid sides and back, boxed, 40 cents.

1. CRANFORD, by Mrs. Gaskell.
2. A WINDOW IN THRUMS, by J. M. Barrie.
3. RAB AND HIS FRIENDS, MARJORIE FLEMING, ETC., by John Brown, M. D.
4. THE VICAR OF WAKEFIELD, by Oliver Goldsmith.
5. THE IDLE THOUGHTS OF AN IDLE FELLOW, by Jerome K. Jerome. "A book for an idle holiday."
6. TALES FROM SHAKSPEARE, by Charles and Mary Lamb, with an introduction by the Rev. Alfred Ainger, M. D.
7. SESAME AND LILIES, by John Ruskin. Three Lectures—I. Of the King's Treasures. II. Of Queen's Garden. III. Of the Mystery of Life.
8. THE ETHICS OF THE DUST, by John Ruskin. Ten lectures to little housewives on the elements of crystalization.
9. THE PLEASURES OF LIFE, by Sir John Lubbock. Complete in one volume.
10. THE SCARLET LETTER, by Nathaniel Hawthorne.
11. THE HOUSE OF THE SEVEN GABLES, by Nathaniel Hawthorne.
12. MOSSES FROM AN OLD MANSE, by Nathaniel Hawthorne.
13. TWICE TOLD TALES, by Nathaniel Hawthorne.
14. THE ESSAYS OF FRANCIS (LORD) BACON WITH MEMOIRS AND NOTES.
15. ESSAYS, First Series, by Ralph Waldo Emerson.
16. ESSAYS, Second Series, by Ralph Waldo Emerson.

HENRY ALTEMUS' PUBLICATIONS.

Altemus' New Illustrated Vademecum Series—Continued.

Price, 40 cents each.

17 REPRESENTATIVE MEN, by Ralph Waldo Emerson. Mental portraits each representing a class. 1. The Philosopher. 2. The Mystic. 3. The Skeptic. 4. The Poet. 5. The Man of the World. 6. The Writer.
18 THOUGHTS OF THE EMPEROR MARCUS AURELIUS ANTONINUS, translated by George Long.
19 THE DISCOURSES OF EPICTETUS WITH THE ENCHIRIDION, translated by George Long.
20 OF THE IMITATION OF CHRIST, by Thomas A'Kempis. Four books complete in one volume.
21 ADDRESSES, by Professor Henry Drummond. The Greatest Thing in the World; Pax Vobiscum; The Changed Life; How to Learn How; Dealing With Doubt; Preparation for Learning; What is a Christian; The Study of the Bible; A Talk on Books.
22 LETTERS, SENTENCES AND MAXIMS, by Lord Chesterfield. Masterpieces of good taste, good writing, and good sense.
23 REVERIES OF A BACHELOR. A book of the heart. By Ik Marvel.
24 DREAM LIFE, by Ik Marvel. A companion to "Reveries of a Bachelor."
25 SARTOR RESARTUS, by Thomas Carlyle.
26 HEROES AND HERO WORSHIP, by Thomas Carlyle.
27 UNCLE TOM'S CABIN, by Harriet Beecher Stowe.
28 ESSAYS OF ELIA, by Charles Lamb.
29 MY POINT OF VIEW. Representative selections from the works of Professor Henry Drummond by William Shepard.
30 THE SKETCH BOOK, by Washington Irving. Complete.
31 KEPT FOR THE MASTER'S USE, by Frances Ridley Havergal.
32 LUCILE, by Owen Meredith.
33 LALLA ROOKH, by Thomas Moore.
34 THE LADY OF THE LAKE, by Sir Walter Scott.
35 MARMION, by Sir Walter Scott.

HENRY ALTEMUS' PUBLICATIONS.

Altemus' New Illustrated Vademecum Series—Continued.
Price, 40 cents each.

36 THE PRINCESS; AND MAUD, by Alfred (Lord) Tennyson.
37 CHILDE HAROLD'S PILGRIMAGE, by Lord Byron.
38 IDYLLS OF THE KING, by Alfred (Lord) Tennyson.
39 EVANGELINE, by Henry Wadsworth Longfellow.
40 VOICES OF THE NIGHT AND OTHER POEMS, by Henry Wadsworth Longfellow.
41 THE BELFRY OF BRUGES AND OTHER POEMS, by Henry Wadsworth Longfellow.
42 THE QUEEN OF THE AIR, by John Ruskin. A study of the Greek myths of cloud and storm.
43 POEMS, Volume I, by John Greenleaf Whittier.
44 POEMS, Volume II, by John Greenleaf Whittier.
45 THE RAVEN; AND OTHER POEMS, by Edgar Allan Poe.
46 THANATOPSIS; AND OTHER POEMS, by William Cullen Bryant.
47 THE LAST LEAF; AND OTHER POEMS, by Oliver Wendell Holmes.
48 THE HEROES OR GREEK FAIRY TALES, by Charles Kingsley.
49 A WONDER BOOK, by Nathaniel Hawthorne.
50 UNDINE, by de La Motte Fouque.
51 ADDRESSES, by the Rt. Rev. Phillips Brooks.
52 BALZAC'S SHORTER STORIES, by Honore de Balzac.
53 TWO YEARS BEFORE THE MAST, by Richard H. Dana, Jr.
54 BENJAMIN FRANKLIN. An autobiography.
55 THE LAST ESSAYS OF ELIA, by Charles Lamb.
56 TOM BROWN'S SCHOOL DAYS, by Thomas Hughes.
57 WEIRD TALES, by Edgar Allen Poe.
58 THE CROWN OF WILD OLIVE, by John Ruskin. Three lectures on Work, Traffic and War.
59 NATURAL LAW IN TE SPIRITUAL WORLD, by Professor Henry Drummond.
60 ABBE CONSTANTIN, by Ludovic Halevy.
61 MANON LESCAUT, by Abbe Prevost.

HENRY ALTEMUS' PUBLICATIONS.

Altemus' New Illustrated Vademecum Series—Continued.
Price, 40 cents each.

62 THE ROMANCE OF A POOR YOUNG MAN, by Octave Feuillet.
63 BLACK BEAUTY, by Anna Sewell.
64 CAMILLE, by Alexander Dumas, Jr.
65 THE LIGHT OF ASIA, by Sir Edwin Arnold.
66 THE LAYS OF ANCIENT ROME, by Thomas Babington Macaulay.
67 THE CONFESSIONS OF AN ENGLISH OPIUM-EATER, by Thomas De Quincey.
68 TREASURE ISLAND, by Robert L. Stevenson.
69 CARMEN, by Prosper Merimee.
70 A SENTIMENTAL JOURNEY, by Laurence Sterne.
71 THE BLITHEDALE ROMANCE, by Nathaniel Hawthorne.
72 BAB BALLADS, AND SAVOY SONGS, by W. H. Gilbert.
73 FANCHON, THE CRICKET, by George Sand.
74 POEMS, by James Russell Lowell.
75 JOHN PLOUGHMANS TALK, by the Rev. Charles H. Spurgeon.
76 JOHN PLOUGHMAN'S PICTURES, by the Rev. Charles H. Spurgeon.
77 THE MANLINESS OF CHRIST, by Thomas Hughes.
78 ADDRESSES TO YOUNG MEN, by the Rev. Henry Ward Beecher.
79 THE AUTOCRAT OF THE BREAKFAST TABLE, by Oliver Wendell Holmes.
80 MULVANEY STORIES, by Rudyard Kipling.
81 BALLADS, by Rudyard Kipling.
82 MORNING THOUGHTS, by Frances Ridley Havergal.
83 TEN NIGHTS IN A BAR ROOM, by T. S. Arthur.
84 EVENING THOUGHTS, by Frances Ridley Havergal.
85 IN MEMORIAM, by Alfred (Lord) Tennyson.
86 COMING TO CHRIST, by Frances Ridley Havergal.
87 HOUSE OF THE WOLF, by Stanley Weyman.

ALTEMUS' ETERNAL LIFE SERIES—Continued.

37. PAX VOBISCUM, by Henry Drummond.
38. THE CHANGED LIFE, by Henry Drummond.
39. FIRST! A TALK WITH BOYS, by Henry Drummond.

ALTEMUS' BELLES-LETTRES SERIES.

A collection of Essays and Addresses by Eminent English and American Authors, beautifully printed and daintily bound, with original designs in silver inks.

Price, 25 cents per volume.

1. INDEPENDENCE DAY, by Rev. Edward E. Hale.
2. THE SCHOLAR IN POLITICS, by Hon. Richard Olney.
3. THE YOUNG MAN IN BUSINESS, by Edward W. Bok.
4. THE YOUNG MAN AND THE CHURCH, by Edward W. Bok.
5. THE SPOILS SYSTEM, by Hon. Carl Schurz.
6. CONVERSATION, by Thomas DeQuincey.
7. SWEETNESS AND LIGHT, by Matthew Arnold.
8. WORK, by John Ruskin.
9. NATURE AND ART, by Ralph Waldo Emerson.
10. THE USE AND MISUSE OF BOOKS, by Frederic Harrison.
11. THE MONROE DOCTRINE: ITS ORIGIN, MEANING AND APPLICATION, by Prof. John Bach McMaster (University of Pennsylvania)
12. THE DESTINY OF MAN, by Sir John Lubbock.
13. LOVE AND FRIENDSHIP, by Ralph Waldo Emerson.
14. RIP VAN WINKLE, by Washington Irving.
15. ART, POETRY AND MUSIC, by Sir John Lubbock.
16. THE CHOICE OF BOOKS, by Sir John Lubbock.
17. MANNERS, by Ralph Waldo Emerson.
18. CHARACTER, by Ralph Waldo Emerson.
19. THE LEGEND OF SLEEPY HOLLOW, by Washington Irving.
20. THE BEAUTIES OF NATURE, by Sir John Lubbock.
21. SELF RELIANCE, by Ralph Waldo Emerson.
22. THE DUTY OF HAPPINESS, by Sir John Lubbock.
23. SPIRITUAL LAWS, by Ralph Waldo Emerson.
24. OLD CHRISTMAS, by Washington Irving.
25. HEALTH, WEALTH AND THE BLESSING OF FRIENDS, by Sir John Lubbock.
26. INTELLECT, by Ralph Waldo Emerson.
27. WHY AMERICANS DISLIKE ENGLAND? by Prof. George B. Adams (Yale).
28. THE HIGHER EDUCATION AS A TRAINING FOR BUSINESS, by Prof. Harry Pratt Judson (University of Chicago).
29. MISS TOOSEY'S MISSION.
30. LADDIE.
31. J. COLE, by Emma Gellibrand.

www.ingramcontent.com/pod-product-compliance
Lightning Source LLC
Chambersburg PA
CBHW020829230426
43666CB00007B/1165